.

THE 90%
ADVANTAGE

THE 90%
ADVANTAGE

How to elevate good people into great performers

Randy Nathan, MA, MSW

C R S
PUBLISHING

CRS Publishing
A Your Personal Coach, LLC Department
www.RandyNathanSpeaks.com

Printed in the United States of America

ISBN – 978-0-9992911-1-5

For Jessa—

My angel who walks beside me every day.
You are my calm in the chaos,
my anchor in the storm, and
my strength when I need it most.

CONTENTS

Acknowledgments 1

Preface 5

CORE PRINCIPLE I:
Mastering the Leadership Mindset

1. The Growth Mindset Advantage............................... 15

2. Effort Drives Growth 33

3. Engaging The Bench Player 59

CORE PRINCIPLE II:
Building Strategic Relationships Beyond the Scoreboard

4. Acceptance in Action: Creating a Positive Culture 85

5. Leading With Empathy 109

6. Learning Through Listening 137

CORE PRINCIPLE III:
Strengthening Resiliency Through Adversity

7. Bouncing Back With Purpose.................................. 163

8. But Can You Pitch 185

9. Small Wins, Big Gains.. 205

Conclusion... 227

ACKNOWLEDGMENTS

This book would not exist without the influence, generosity, and outright brilliance of my friend, colleague, and longtime guru, **David Avrin**. I've known David since high school, and he has been a true inspiration ever since. His international speaking success, thought leadership, and bestselling books—most recently *Ridiculously Easy to Do Business With*—lit a path I've aspired to follow. When I declared 2025 as my year of transition from youth sports and education into the world of business and corporate speaking, David invited me to his book-writing retreat—a turning point that sparked the creation of this book. He helped shape the title, connected me with my editor, designer, layout expert, and printer, and—despite his packed schedule—still made time for my texts, calls, and Zoom sessions. To say I admire him would be an understatement. If I achieve even half of what he has accomplished, I'll consider myself incredibly successful. Thank you, David, for being a generous mentor and a constant example of what's possible.

Right alongside that inspiration is my dearest and closest friend, **Adam Shandler**—my brother from another mother. His willingness to read my second draft and offer thoughtful, experienced feedback as an HR executive was a godsend. Adam brought a sharp lens, honest reactions, and a supportive voice exactly when I needed it. Beyond the book, our friendship—strengthened over countless New Year's Eve celebrations and unforgettable trips to the Outer Banks—has been one of the greatest constants in my life.

I'm forever grateful for the bond we share and the insight he brings, both professionally and personally.

To the **clients, colleagues, schools, companies, and organizations** who have invited me to speak over the past 20 years—you helped build the foundation for this book. Whether I was leading a workshop in a boardroom, presenting in a school auditorium, or Zooming into a team meeting from my kitchen, you gave me a platform, a purpose, and an audience. Every question you asked, every conversation we shared, and every story you told shaped the lessons and insights in these pages. Thank you for allowing me to learn from you while doing what I love.

To my editor, **Barry Lyons**, thank you for being the voice of reason and refinement. Your ability to guide the manuscript with professionalism, insight, and a sense of humor made this process more collaborative than I could've imagined. You didn't just clean up sentences—you helped elevate the entire message.

To **Ajmer Singh**, who took a manuscript and made it into a beautiful book—thank you for your patience, precision, and design expertise. Every layout decision, every formatting choice, and every late-night tweak helped bring this project to life with clarity and style.

To my **dad**, your unwavering support and generosity have been a lifeline to my future. Your belief in me, especially as I chose to pivot directions with my company, means more than I can ever express. Thank you for providing the space and resources for me to learn, grow, and invest in myself through this journey. Your dedication has been foundational to this new chapter in my life.

To my children—**Jess and her husband Jonny, Alex, Mikayla, and Brianna**—I have always tried to be the best father I could be. I know I've stumbled at times, but everything I've done has been rooted in love and a desire to see you thrive. This book is more than just a leadership message—it's my personal hope for each of you: that you rise up, embrace your 90%, and become champions for those around you who may go unnoticed. I love you more than words can hold, and I am forever grateful and humbled that I get to be your dad.

To my wife Jessa, **my best friend, my partner, my angel**. From the moment you unexpectedly walked into my life, you've brought light, steadiness, and love in ways I never saw coming. You are the most influential, most important, and most meaningful person in my life. You are not only an incredible wife and mother to our daughters, but you are also a force in your own right—an inspiration as an educator, a leader, and a friend to so many. Your support has been my anchor, and your strength my motivation. I love you to the moon and back, the stars and back, *thrice*. Always have. Always will.

And to **you**, the reader, thank you for stepping into these pages. If this book made you think differently about leadership, reminded you of someone quietly carrying the team, or sparked an idea to uplift the overlooked, then it did its job.

The truth is, you don't need to be the MVP to make a difference. You just need to recognize the 90% around you—the steady, the committed, and the often invisible backbone of every organization—and lead like they matter. Because they do.

"I'm in the twilight of a mediocre career…I've had more numbers on my back than a bingo board."

— Rocky Bridges, MLB utility player

PREFACE

The Unsung Heroes – The 90% Advantage

In our earliest memories of school, a message is ingrained in us: excellence equals success. The report card becomes our first scoreboard, and the coveted "A" is not just a grade; it's a validation, a stepping stone, a necessity. "Get good grades," they say, "and you'll get into a great college." The promise continues: "Get into a great college, and you'll land a great job. Land a great job, and you'll make a lot of money. Make a lot of money, and you'll be happy and successful." Somewhere in this sequence, nobody mentions how many cups of coffee, late nights, and mini-crises you'll endure along the way.

> *"This script doesn't just fade away after graduation. It's like glitter—you think it's gone, but it's stuck in the carpet of your soul forever."*

This script doesn't just fade away after graduation. It's like glitter—you think it's gone, but it's stuck in the carpet of your soul forever. The pressure to be exceptional doesn't just continue; it gets a corner office. As employees, we're expected to hit impossible deadlines, innovate like Steve Jobs, and still remember everyone's birthday. As managers, the stakes double. Now, you're supposed to inspire excellence in your team, solve problems before they happen, and lead meetings that don't make people want to fake a Wi-Fi outage. The scoreboard evolves, but the rules remain the same: keep winning or risk becoming invisible.

Yet, the reality for most of us profoundly differs from the glossy, Instagram-worthy ideal we've been sold. Despite our best efforts, we don't all become CEOs or get fan mail for our PowerPoint presentations. We don't grace magazine covers or retire with fortunes so vast they'd make a lottery winner jealous. Instead, most of us live lives of quiet determination, contributing in ways that will never go viral—unless you count the time you accidentally replied-all to the company email.

I believed in this blueprint for most of my life. Until life decided to get creative, throw me a curveball, and knock me flat on my back. Picture this: I was divorced, suddenly the single parent of a two-and-a-half-year-old and a sixteen-month-old. As if that wasn't enough, I got fired—twice. My mother and brother both passed away unexpectedly, leaving me reeling. Life didn't just throw bricks at me; it delivered them in bulk. Everything I was taught and conditioned myself to believe fell apart like a poorly made IKEA shelf. My world spun out of control, and I was left standing in the rubble, wondering if I'd missed some fine print on the blueprint for life.

But here's the thing about tailspins: eventually, you find your bearings. Over time, I adapted. I learned. I overcame. I remarried. I realized that life's unexpected challenges don't just knock you down; they shape you into someone who knows how to stand back up—even if it's wobbly at first. I changed. This is what I learned.

I am a father first, a husband second, and a coach third. In that order. Why? Because there are only so many "dad jokes" a man can unleash before facing the music and admitting his true identity. If you're anything like me, you spend more time than you'd care to admit pondering life's big, existential questions: Who am I? Where am I going? And, how do I get there without opening another tab in Google Maps?

Everything I do—every choice, action, and slightly cringey joke—is anchored in one unshakable priority: my family. For as long as I can remember, my life has been guided by this internal compass, pointing me toward creating a legacy my kids might someday look at and say, "Wow, Dad actually knew what he was doing."

> *"Most of us live lives of quiet determination, contributing in ways that will never go viral— unless you count the time you accidentally replied-all to the company email."*

Whether it's authoring a book, delivering a keynote, or teaching a class, all roads have led me to this moment—this book. If my life were a movie (we're talking more underdog sports film than sleek Hollywood thriller), this book would be the slow-motion scene where the underdog finally hits their stride. Instead of catching a touchdown, I'm catching your attention—and maybe even helping you catch your breath as you navigate the fast-paced world of work, leadership, and organizational challenges.

There is a clear and compelling connection between those who have competed in sports and their success in leadership and business opportunities. Fortune estimates that an astounding 95% of Fortune 500 CEOs played sports at some point in their lives. The pattern holds true among women leaders—while only 6% of Fortune 500 CEOs are women, a study by Ernst & Young found that 90% of high-level female executives played competitive sports. But it's not just athletes who reap these benefits. The same holds true for those who participated in school plays, marched in the drumline, or led debate teams. These extra-curricular experiences provided life lessons and leadership opportunities that traditional classrooms simply couldn't.

Back then, our goals were ambitious. We aimed for the D1 scholarship, dreamed of performing on Broadway, or envisioned ourselves playing first-chair French horn at Carnegie Hall. Our parents invested thousands of dollars in lessons, training, and support—fueling our passion and commitment. We traveled hundreds of miles, woke up before dawn, returned home long after dark, and spent weekends in less-than-glamorous hotels, all in pursuit of excellence.

Now, those days exist only as cherished memories—moments from a time that shaped us but often feel distant. Yet, deep within the core of who we are, those experiences have built a foundation that prepared us for the challenges of today. But something feels off. Life has marched forward, and perhaps your passion, drive, or competitive edge has faded somewhere along the way. Your empathy towards others may have diminished. The work you once found fulfilling now seems routine, and the staff around you—

disconnected, disengaged—also realize that the blueprint they were given for success isn't as clear or sustainable as they once believed.

The truth is, instead of the MVPs we aspired to be, we've all become everyday players and team members. But it doesn't have to be that way. Every team member holds value. And the lessons we learned from our past experiences can reignite the fire within us. Whether in the boardroom, on the front lines, or behind the scenes, your contributions—and those of your team—can make all the difference. It's time to tap back into that passion, rediscover the drive, and lead with purpose again.

We often find ourselves searching for the next big win—the promotion, the major deal, the standout achievement that validates our efforts. But true success isn't built on a single defining moment; it's forged through the consistency of smaller, often unnoticed contributions. In these moments—often overlooked or undervalued—the real magic happens.

The NFL has a storied history filled with highlight-reel touchdowns, bone-crushing tackles, and miraculous comebacks. But behind the glamour of the long passes and the crowd's roar lies a quieter hero: the field goal. Over the years, thousands of NFL games have been decided by the simple, unassuming act of sending a football through the uprights. A field goal has won over 1,700 games since the league's inception.

Yet, during the ebb and flow of a game, field goals are often perceived as a consolation prize. A compromise. The offense stalls, unable to find the end zone, and the field goal unit jogs onto the field to "settle." For fans, it's a collective sigh, not a roar. The scoreboard moves, but the energy doesn't. A field goal is functional, not flashy. It's the reliable coworker who shows up on time, does their job, and rarely makes headlines.

But when the game is on the line, everything changes. Suddenly, that "meh" moment becomes the center of the universe. In those final seconds, the kicker—a player many fans couldn't name—becomes the hero or the villain. The weight of an entire team's efforts and a season's dreams can rest on the swing of one leg. The roar of the crowd crescendos, millions hold their breath, and the ball sails into history—either through the uprights or agonizingly wide.

A similar dynamic occurs on the diamond with baseball, another underappreciated skill: the bunt. The bunt rarely gets the spotlight in a sport defined by towering home runs and strikeout artists. But to those who truly understand the game, a well-executed bunt can change everything. The sacrifice moves a runner into scoring position, the strategic play that shifts the momentum, or the surprise element rattling a defense.

Sports isn't the only stage where the unsung hero quietly carries the weight of success. Maybe you weren't scoring touchdowns but hitting high notes in the choir, marching with the band, or perfecting your jazz hands in theater class. Whether you were belting it out in the Glee Club or harmonizing in the choir, the motto was always the same: "One band, one sound. One song, one voice." And while the spotlight may have shone on the leads, let's face it, without the ensemble, the show would be a total flop.

In the workplace, disengagement is an epidemic that quietly undermines businesses and stifles potential. According to Gallup's "State of the Workplace 2024" report, a staggering 62% of employees globally are not engaged—they show up, do the bare minimum, and remain emotionally detached from their roles and organizations. Even more concerning, 15% of workers are actively disengaged, harboring resentment that can actively work against company progress.[1]

In addition, the desire for change is more than just a passing trend. It's a loud and clear signal that employees seek something more from their careers. A recent survey by ResumeTemplates.com reveals that 56% of full-time employees in the U.S. are looking for a new job in 2025, with over a quarter already actively searching.[2]

These unsung heroes are the backbone of every organization. They also yearn for someone to believe in them, much like their high school coach, drama director, or orchestra conductor. Without effective leadership, meaningful engagement strategies, and a culture that fosters growth and recognition, businesses risk losing productivity and the very people who can make a real difference when given the right support.

That's the core of The 90% Advantage. This book is built on Three Core Principles:

1. Mastering the Leadership Mindset
2. Building Strategic Relationships Beyond the Scoreboard
3. Strengthening Resiliency Through Adversity

---

1   https://stylus.com/consumer-attitudes/gallup-s-state-of-the-workplace-2024-global-workers-disengaged

2   https://www.inc.com/annabel-burba/6-in-10-employees-want-a-new-job-in-2025/90996777

These aren't just abstract ideas. They are your practical playbook for success, helping you cultivate clarity, harness collaboration, and build the mental toughness needed to thrive.

CORE PRINCIPLE I

Mastering the Leadership Mindset

"You can't put a limit on anything.
The more you dream, the farther you get."

— Michael Phelps

1.

The Growth Mindset Advantage

It would be both impossible and unethical to discuss the concept of a growth mindset without acknowledging the pioneering work of Carol Dweck—renowned psychologist, Stanford University researcher, and author of Mindset: The New Psychology of Success. Every generation is gifted with thought leaders who introduce groundbreaking ideas that challenge how we perceive the world, creating a ripple effect that transforms our understanding and behavior. Their insights are so profound yet intuitive that they leave us wondering, Why didn't I think of that?

Consider the timeless influence of Napoleon Hill, whose Think and Grow Rich continues to inspire success seekers, or Dale Carnegie, whose How to Win Friends and Influence People revolutionized interpersonal relationships. More recently, Stephen Covey's The 7 Habits of Highly Effective People and Jim Collins's Good to Great have reshaped leadership and organizational effectiveness. These authors have introduced ideas that fundamentally alter how we approach our personal and professional lives.

Carol Dweck undoubtedly belongs to this esteemed group of transformative thinkers. Her work on mindset has reshaped educational and corporate landscapes and provided individuals with a powerful framework to unlock their potential and achieve lasting success. She explores how our beliefs about intelligence and abilities shape our success and growth. She introduces two key mindsets: fixed and growth. A fixed mindset assumes abilities are unchangeable, leading to avoidance of challenges and fear of failure.

In contrast, a growth mindset sees abilities as adaptable through effort and perseverance, fostering resilience and a love of learning. Dweck shows how adopting a growth mindset can unlock potential and lead to meaningful success. The book offers practical strategies to shift perspectives, embrace challenges, and persist through setbacks, ultimately providing a powerful framework for personal and professional development.

Understanding the power of mindset is crucial in addressing the widespread dissatisfaction in today's workforce. While external factors such as workplace culture and leadership play significant roles, employees' internal beliefs about their abilities and potential are just as important. Carol Dweck's groundbreaking research highlights how shifting from a fixed to a growth mindset can catalyze renewed motivation and engagement. Employees who believe their skills and talents can evolve through effort will likely embrace challenges, seek development opportunities, and find fulfillment in their roles. By fostering a culture that nurtures a growth mindset, leaders can reduce turnover and empower their workers to thrive in the face of change.

This is the first step of maximizing the 90% advantage. The everyday employees. Those who are not flashy MVPs make up most of any organization's workforce. These individuals often come to work with the desire to contribute, but they can become disillusioned without proper guidance. As leaders, we have a unique opportunity to nurture their potential by cultivating a growth mindset across our teams. When managers coach, encourage, and invest in these good people, they can develop into exceptional performers, driving long-term success for themselves and the organization. The true competitive advantage lies in elevating the 90% who quietly hold the business together.

Your Mind

At some point in the past 20 years, give or take a few questionable fashion choices, I recall a thought-provoking question: What is the one thing you have that no one else has unless you give it away? I'd love to say I remember exactly where I heard it. Maybe it was during a keynote presentation, a workshop, or perhaps while diving deep into Napoleon Hill's Think and Grow Rich. Or, it may have been while half-listening to his CD collection of lectures during one of my ambitious phases. You know, one of those moments when you convince yourself that personal growth pairs well with rush-hour traffic.

Regardless, the question stuck with me. Phrased differently, it could be: What is the one thing you have that no one else can take unless you willingly hand it over? What is your answer? What do you think? Your first thoughts may be pretty basic, your Netflix password, the last pizza slice, your secret emergency chocolate stash. Are you able to solve the riddle? Or does it have to be spelled out for you? The answer is plainly obvious.

The answer is your mind.

Your mind is the one thing that truly belongs to you. No one else has it, no one else can replicate it, and no one else can take it unless you let them. Even identical twins, triplets, or quadruplets, who might look like carbon copies, each possess a unique mind. Sure, they may share DNA, but what are their thoughts, perspectives, and internal narratives? Completely different. Your mind is a one-of-a-kind blend of life experiences, lessons learned (sometimes the hard way), cherished memories, and deeply held beliefs. It's the engine that drives you forward, the brake that stops you when needed, and the voice inside your head that whispers (or sometimes shouts) advice when you're facing a tough choice.

Your mind is, without a doubt, the core component of who you are. Yet, ironically, it's the first thing we tend to surrender, often without even realizing it. We hand it over to the relentless demands of work, the expectations of others, and the constant bombardment of distractions that multiply faster than emails in your inbox. Whether it's saying "yes" to every meeting that could've been an email, falling down the rabbit hole of social media doom-scrolling, or letting someone else's stress hijack your own mood, your mind—your most valuable asset—gets given away far too easily.

And once it's gone? Reclaiming it can feel like trying to cancel a gym membership: frustrating, time-consuming, and often requiring a level of persistence you weren't quite prepared for. Whether it's in your career, relationships, or even those precious few moments of downtime, how well you manage and protect your mind is what ultimately determines your success, happiness, and, let's be honest, your sanity.

So, the next time you find yourself overwhelmed, stretched too thin, or wondering why you're spending more time managing other people's priorities than your own, ask yourself: Who did I give my mind to today? And more importantly, how do I get it back?

Your Inner Drive

What gets you out of bed every morning? Is it the thrill of a new day or just the dread of an alarm clock that feels like it goes off five minutes after you fell asleep? Why do you endure the daily commute, braving traffic jams? If you're working remotely, why do you fight the urge to stay in your pajamas and turn on your computer?

So, what fuels you? Mondays will always feel like an ambush if you don't know.

Maybe your drive is simple: the paycheck. The lifeblood that keeps the lights on, funds that dream vacation, and ensures your fridge isn't just a storage space for expired condiments. Or maybe it runs deeper, you still believe you can make a difference. You cling to the idea that your work, skills, and persistence can create an impact, whether in the office, on a Zoom call, or in the little victories that keep your career moving forward. You're building a future, maintaining a family, and securing a legacy—one email, project, and coffee break at a time.

What fuels the people around you? Your staff? Your colleagues? Your boss? Understanding their internal drive isn't just a fun guessing game; it's the key to unlocking better teamwork, stronger relationships, and a more engaged workplace. Everyone has a reason for showing up. The better you understand those reasons, the better you can lead, support, and connect.

When speaking with athletes, I often ask, "Why do you play sports?" It's not just a conversation starter. It's the most important question of my keynote. If an adult or coach is in the room, without fail, one of the first responses is, "I want to win." And honestly, that makes perfect sense. After all, isn't that what sports are all about? The thrill of victory, the satisfaction of outperforming your opponent, and the glory of being the best? Winning feels good. No argument there.

But when I ask the same question in a room full of just athletes, whether a high school volleyball team or a college basketball program, their answers are refreshingly simple and, quite frankly, a little surprising. "To have fun." That's it. No deep strategic analysis, no talk of championships or records—just the pure, unfiltered joy of the game. Because at its core, sports are supposed to be fun. That's why we all start in the first place—running around a field as kids, laughing with friends, and feeling the rush of simply playing.

Yet, something happens along the way. As athletes age, the competition becomes fiercer, and the pressure to win creeps in—from coaches, parents, teammates, and even themselves. Suddenly, the joy of the game takes a back seat to the relentless pursuit of victory. The fun that once fueled their passion gets overshadowed by performance metrics, scholarship opportunities, and the looming fear of failure. The "win at all costs" mentality starts to take hold, and soon, sports feel more like a job than a passion.

And while the drive to win is natural, there's a fine line between healthy competition and letting it consume everything. When winning becomes the only focus, the love for the game starts to fade, burnout sets in, and the very reason they started playing in the first place—fun—is lost in the shuffle.

> *"While the drive to win is natural, there's a fine line between healthy competition and letting it consume everything."*

This mindset and relentless pursuit of winning don't just stay confined to the court or the field. It has a sneaky way of planting roots and festering in every corner of our lives. It seeps into our work, infecting our teams, our culture, and the overall vibe of our professional lives. And it doesn't stop there. It quietly infiltrates our marriages, families, and—perhaps most terrifying—our parenting styles. Suddenly, bedtime routines feel like negotiating high-stakes contracts, and family game night turns into a cutthroat competition worthy of a reality TV show.

There is absolutely nothing wrong with wanting to win. Striving to win can be a powerful motivator. It drives innovation, pushes us to improve, and keeps us from getting too comfortable. But when everything in life starts to feel like a must-win scenario, we risk losing control over our lives when we measure our success by some invisible scoreboard or random algorithm. We start living in an exhausting all-or-nothing cycle where every project, every conversation, and every decision feels like a championship game. And let's be honest: no one can live like that without eventually burning out—or worse, losing sight of what truly matters.

Before we know it, we've handed over the keys to our happiness, our well-being, and even our identities to this relentless pursuit of success. Your inner drive isn't about being the best at everything or constantly pushing yourself to exhaustion. It's about finding the deeper purpose that fuels you. The thing that gets you moving beyond just deadlines and expectations. Your drive is personal, powerful, and uniquely yours. It's not defined by promotions, paychecks, or social media highlight reels. It's about what truly matters to you. Whether providing for your family, making a difference in your community, or simply finding joy in what you do, your drive must serve as your compass, not your scoreboard.

So, instead of getting caught up in the endless chase, please take a moment to reconnect with it. Because when you align your actions with your true drive, success stops being a race and starts becoming a journey worth taking.

What's getting in the way of your drive? What sneaky little forces are causing you to hand over control of your mind like it's a free giveaway at a trade show? What obstacles or challenges stand between you and your best version—the ultimate you? As an executive coach, I see it all the time, and I can tell you this with absolute certainty: the biggest thing standing between you and your goals...is you.

True, there are external factors that can trip you up. I'm a solid 5'8" on a good day, which means no matter how much I dream, train, or believe in myself, I will never be the next NBA superstar. However, Muggsy Bogues, who stood at just 5'3", carved out a remarkable 14-year career in the NBA. He defied every expectation, played with heart, speed, and hustle, and became one of the most respected point guards in the league. He even made his way to the big screen with a starring role in the original Space Jam alongside Michael Jordan, holding his own both in the paint and Hollywood. Bogues didn't let height define his limits. He rewrote the playbook.

While external obstacles can certainly slow us down, our biggest challenge is usually our fear. And fear is the ultimate shape-shifter. It can disguise itself as self-doubt, procrastination, or that little voice whispering, "Maybe tomorrow." Legendary speaker Zig Ziglar once said that fear stands for "False Evidence Appearing Real," and he was onto something. We let fear trick us into believing in limitations that don't exist, convincing ourselves that success is only for the lucky or the talented.

But fear isn't some immovable mountain. It's all about how you choose to see it. You can let it control you, dictate your choices, and hold you hostage—or you can call its bluff and take the first step forward. The good news is, you don't have to climb that mountain all at once or alone. Moving past fear starts with small, intentional actions. Say yes to the uncomfortable meeting, raise your hand when unsure, and ask the question no one else wants to voice. Action breeds momentum, and momentum turns hesitation into progress. You don't need to be fearless. You need to be willing. Fear may not disappear, but it loses its grip when you decide to move.

Because more often than not, the only thing truly stopping you...is you.

The Advantage

The growth mindset is like having a mental remote control. You get to decide what channel your thoughts tune into. It strengthens you by helping you see that every experience, whether riding high on success or trudging through failure, is a chance to learn and grow. After all, life is a perceptual illusion; it's all about how you choose to see it. What sparks fear in one person might ignite excitement in another. Some see failure as the end. Others see it as a valuable lesson wrapped in disguise and frustration.

Conversely, a fixed mindset clings to believing leaders are born, not made. If you buy into that idea and do not see yourself as someone capable of leadership, you will likely never even approach the challenge. But here is the good news. Embracing a growth mindset means realizing leadership is a skill, not a birthright. Every choice you make, every setback you encounter, and every victory you celebrate is a stepping stone toward becoming the leader you aspire to be.

Although we will dive deeper into this later in the book, one of the most significant advantages of adopting a growth mindset is how it transforms your relationship with change. In today's whirlwind world, the only thing you can truly count on is not knowing what is coming next. Those with a fixed mindset often see unexpected challenges as terrifying monsters lurking around every corner. With a growth mindset, those same challenges become exciting plot twists in your success story. Change is not the enemy. It is the opportunity you have been waiting for. Setbacks are not brick walls. They are stepping stones disguised as learning opportunities.

When you embrace growth, flexibility, and optimism, they become your go-to tools. They help you conquer whatever life throws your way.

Leadership is not a solo mission. Those who believe in growth tend to foster workplaces and communities that thrive on collaboration instead of cutthroat competition. Instead of viewing coworkers as rivals in some epic office showdown, they see them as teammates working toward a common goal. Feedback? Bring it on. Different perspectives? Even better. Growth-minded leaders are the ones building bridges, not burning them. They communicate openly, tackle conflict with a "let's figure this out" attitude instead of defensiveness, and create a culture where everyone can thrive.

At the end of the day, a growth mindset is not just good for you. It is contagious. It spreads success and stronger connections wherever it goes.

Now that you have tapped into your inner drive, sharpened your vision, and developed a newfound appreciation (and hopefully a burning desire) to embrace a growth mindset, you are officially ready to level up. It's like upgrading from a basic toolkit to the deluxe, all-the-bells-and-whistles version. You are no longer just dipping your toes into the waters of potential. You are diving in, ready to swim laps.

Embracing a growth mindset is not just about nodding along to inspiring ideas. It's about rolling up your sleeves and putting them into action. You have the foundation, the motivation, and the spark. It is time to use them to elevate yourself and the people around you.

> *"You are no longer just dipping your toes into the waters of potential. You are diving in, ready to swim laps."*

This is where the 90% advantage comes to life. Authentic leadership is not about being the loudest voice or the star performer. It's about recognizing and nurturing the potential in those who consistently show up, work hard, and seek to grow. These everyday contributors are your greatest asset. You are not just building a stronger team when you help them unlock their hidden strengths and level up. You are creating a competitive advantage that sets your organization apart.

Take a deep breath. Square your shoulders. Get ready.

Because the next chapter is not just another page; it is your next big step toward elevating yourself and everyone around you into greatness.

A CASE STUDY

QUEST DIAGNOSTICS – THE CALL CENTER TURNAROUND

Quest Diagnostics, a leading provider of diagnostic services in the United States, faced significant challenges in its National Customer Service (NCS) organization. Following the consolidation of 20 customer service call centers into two, the company grappled with high labor costs, absenteeism, and turnover. Customer dissatisfaction was on the rise, with some clients turning to competitors. In July 2015, MaryAnn Camacho was appointed as the Executive Director of NCS to spearhead a turnaround. Camacho recognized that an overemphasis on productivity metrics had led supervisors to prioritize call volume over effective issue resolution, trapping the organization in a negative feedback loop. She contemplated whether to focus first on people or operations to address these issues.[3]

Using a growth mindset MaryAnn Camacho implemented several key initiatives to transform NCS:[4]

1. Investing in Employees:

Camacho increased starting wages and established a step-based pay system, creating clear career paths for employees. This investment aimed to reduce turnover and enhance employee satisfaction.

---

3   https://mitsloan.mit.edu/teaching-resources-library/quest-diagnostics-a-improving-performance-call-centers
4   https://goodjobsinstitute.org/portfolio/good-job-strategy-at-quest-diagnostics

2. Operational Improvements:

She standardized processes and empowered employees through cross-training, enabling them to handle a broader range of tasks. This approach improved efficiency and service quality.

3. Employee Empowerment:

Camacho fostered a culture of continuous improvement by encouraging employees to contribute ideas and take ownership of their roles, leading to increased engagement and performance.

As a result of these strategic initiatives, employee turnover plummeted by an impressive 50%, significantly reducing the costly cycle of recruitment and training. This drastic improvement lowered direct turnover expenses and fostered a more stable and experienced workforce. The impact on career development was equally profound: promotion rates skyrocketed, tripling as employees seized newfound opportunities for growth and advancement within the company. Perhaps most importantly, the focus on employee development and operational enhancements ignited a cultural transformation, boosting morale and engagement to unprecedented levels. Employees felt valued, empowered, and motivated to contribute meaningfully, driving both individual and organizational success.

CULTIVATING A GROWTH MINDSET CULTURE

Here are five strategic ways to lead with a growth mindset and unlock untapped potential across your team:

- **Coach the process, not just the outcome.** Encourage effort, strategy, and improvement over perfection. Praise persistence and adaptability as much as results.

- **Shift the language.** Swap out fixed mindset phrases like "You're a natural" with growth-oriented feedback such as "Your hard work is paying off." What leaders say becomes what teams believe.

- **Normalize learning curves.** Create psychological safety by sharing your own failures and what they taught you. When leaders admit they're still learning, it gives everyone permission to do the same.

- **Ask future-focused questions.** In one-on-ones or team meetings, regularly ask: "What are you working on getting better at?" or "What's one thing you learned this week?" It reinforces improvement as a core expectation.

- **Invest in the 90%.** Provide coaching, training, and opportunities to those who show up and try—even if they aren't the flashiest players. The real advantage comes from elevating the reliable, not just rewarding the remarkable.

When leaders embrace the power of "yet," they invite a culture of resilience, learning, and long-term excellence.

The growth mindset isn't a buzzword. It's a leadership lens that changes how you see your people and what they believe is possible.

"Even if you're on the right track, you'll get run over if you just sit there."

— Will Rogers

2.

Effort Drives Growth

Louis was a lively and talkative young boy with a big personality—and an even bigger problem. His thoughts didn't just come quietly; they bubbled inside him like a volcano ready to blow. And when they did, BOOM! Out they came, interrupting conversations at the worst possible moments, whether it was during class discussions, his mom's phone calls, or when his friends were mid-sentence. He wasn't trying to be rude; he couldn't help it. In his mind, every thought was too important to wait. But, much to his surprise, not everyone shared his sense of urgency.

Eventually, Louis's constant interruptions started to test the patience of those around him. His teacher gave him "the look," his parents tried gentle reminders (and not-so-gentle ones), and even his friends were getting annoyed. Still, Louis couldn't hold it in. Then, one fateful day, his friends started interrupting him. And suddenly, he got it. Being cut off wasn't fun at all.

Bedtime in my house was sacred when my children were young. Amidst the day's chaos, spilled juice, endless errands, and deadlines, it was the one time I could hit pause, snuggle up, and focus on what mattered: my kids. And Louis was a frequent bedtime guest in the form of My Mouth Is a Volcano by Julia Cook. This charming story isn't just about a kid with an overactive mouth; it's about self-control, patience, and learning the art of waiting your turn. Louis learns that while his thoughts are important, managing his impulses and respecting others is even more so.

Louis wants to change, but it takes time. Real, honest-to-goodness effort. He has to practice deep breathing, pausing, and learning when not to explode (a skill many adults could use too). This story is a perfect example of how growth doesn't come from instant perfection but from steady, determined improvement. Whether it's learning to wait your turn in class, improving relationships, or striving for professional success, effort is what makes the difference.

Now, take a step back and think about your own life. Consider your job, your responsibilities, and everything that seems to go haywire on a daily basis. Think about the things that are not in your control—like traffic, that painfully slow elevator, or the Wi-Fi deciding to take the day off when you need it most. The list of things out of your control is, unfortunately, endless.

> *"Realizing that attitude and effort are the only things in our control can be a game-changer."*

But what is in your control? That's where things get interesting. As much as we'd love to believe we can control everything (or everyone), the truth is that we can only control two things: our attitude and our effort. That's it. Not even our mind is entirely under our command. If you've ever found yourself worrying at 2:00 a.m. about whether you replied to that email, you know exactly what I mean.

Our minds have a mind of their own, stirring up fear, frustration, and really great responses to a conversation from three years ago.

Realizing that attitude and effort are the only things in our control can be a game-changer. Whether you're an athlete, a leader, or just trying to survive Monday mornings, mastering these two areas can make life much easier. So why waste energy stressing over things beyond your control? Instead, channel that energy into what you can control: your mindset and your daily effort. Because when you finally accept this reality, life becomes a whole lot simpler (and maybe even a little more fun).

The Scoreboard Mentality

There is no shortage of quotes about winning in sports. You've probably heard them all: "No one remembers second place." "Winning isn't everything; it's the only thing." And the ever-motivational, "Show me a good loser, and I'll show you a loser." These phrases get tossed around like confetti at a championship parade, drilling the idea into our heads that winning is the only ultimate goal.

Our obsession with winning is practically Pavlovian. Ring a bell and get a treat. Win a game, and you're showered with applause, high-fives, and maybe even a free meal. Lose? Well, expect an earful from your coach, your parents, and that one overzealous fan who thinks they could have done better from their recliner. Determining which feels better doesn't take a genius—winning or losing. Let's say it's not losing.

This deep-seated conditioning doesn't stop on the field; it follows us everywhere: in boardrooms, sales floors, and even backyard BBQs where someone inevitably turns a casual game of cornhole into the Super Bowl. The scoreboard mentality runs the show. In sports, the scoreboard is king. Players watch it, coaches obsess over it, and spectators can't take their eyes off it. And it's not just the game they're watching. It's all the games. Have you ever watched a sporting event, and someone new enters the room? The first question they ask is, "What's the score?" Maybe they'll ask, "Who's playing?" but, realistically, the score is what they "really" want to know. We are absolutely, undeniably obsessed with the numbers on that board.

What is very funny is when coaches of little kids' teams announce, with a straight face, that they're "not going to keep score" during the game. Yeah, sure. As if that's going to fly. The idea is noble. Teaching kids that the score doesn't define their experience. But here's the funny part: those same kids go home and watch their parents lose their minds over the score of a football game on TV, high-fiving each other, yelling at referees through the screen, and meticulously tracking their Fantasy Football points like it's Wall Street. And the kids? They're taking notes. They're watching, absorbing, and—surprise, surprise—keeping score anyway. If you think a group of 8-year-olds can't keep track of goals or baskets independently, you've seriously underestimated their math skills. The reality is that they know the truth. The score always matters, whether we admit it or not.

The scoreboard mentality prioritizes visible, quantifiable results over everything else, often at the expense of long-term growth, learning, and well-being. At its core, it's an obsession with results. It's all about what you achieved, not how you got there. Did you hit the numbers? Close the deals? Win the game? If not? There is no next time. This relentless focus on outcomes leaves little room for learning, experimentation, or progress that isn't immediately measurable.

Comparison is another key component. Success isn't just about your performance; it's about beating the competition. Whether it's other teams, colleagues, or even social media connections posting their suspiciously perfect LinkedIn updates, everyone is constantly measured against each other. "Am I better than them?" becomes the driving force, leading to unhealthy competition and unnecessary stress. This pressure creates a deep fear of mistakes. In a scoreboard mentality, mistakes equal losses, and losses equal consequences. The result? People avoid risks, play it safe, and innovation takes a backseat because no one wants to be the one responsible for a bad quarter or a missed goal.

Adding to the problem is the short-term focus that the scoreboard mentality breeds. Long-term strategy? Forget it. The focus is on immediate gratification—what are the numbers right now? This creates an environment of constant crunch time, where today's performance outweighs sustainable success. Alongside this, the need for external validation becomes addictive. If it's not on the scoreboard, it didn't happen. Winning is great, but what's even better? Everyone knows you won. Whether it's social media posts, trophy pictures, or celebratory emails, the scoreboard mentality craves recognition and applause.

This all-or-nothing thinking leaves no room for a middle ground. You're either a winner or a loser—no "good effort" category exists. Such pressure often leads to burnout and a lack of appreciation for small, incremental wins. Additionally, overemphasizing quantifiable metrics means that if something can't be measured, it doesn't matter. Soft skills, teamwork, and resilience? Nice to have, but the scoreboard only cares about numbers, percentages, and hard data. This can create an environment where intangible contributions are overlooked, and real leadership development is stifled.

Finally, the scoreboard mentality creates constant pressure to perform. Whether it's in business, sports, or life, people feel they must be "on" all the time. Taking a break or slowing down can feel like falling behind, leading to exhaustion and disengagement. While the scoreboard mentality seems like a powerful motivator, it comes at a high cost. The challenge lies in understanding that the scoreboard becomes a trap. After all, no one wants to spend their whole life staring at the scoreboard only to realize they've been playing the wrong game all along.

That's the power of the 90% advantage. Instead of obsessing over immediate wins, leaders can learn to focus on developing the majority of their team. It's this effort, often overshadowed by scoreboard pressure, that transforms businesses and careers. Winning matters, sure. However, learning how to value and leverage the process of growth matters even more. By shifting focus to developing and supporting those incremental gains, leaders unlock the true advantage: sustainable success driven by engaged, capable performers who turn everyday effort into exceptional results.

A large portion of companies rely on competition to motivate staff, often through tools like the "Leader Board." Much like a sports scoreboard, the leaderboard shines a bright spotlight on results, pushing employees to hit their numbers, perform at a high level, and achieve tangible outcomes. But it's usually the same two or three people who dominate the top spots every time. Meanwhile, those who consistently put in strong effort but fall short of making the board begin to feel invisible. Their contributions don't count, no matter how hard they work. Or worse, they miss out on that coveted trip to Cancun. And slowly, they begin to lose motivation.

Over time, these employees, realizing that their effort goes unnoticed and unrewarded, start to dial it back. They do just enough to get by, slipping into "paycheck mode." They do the job, but far from their best. Without recognition or opportunities for meaningful growth, their performance plateaus. These are often the people with untapped potential, the organization's backbone, who could achieve far more if given the right support and encouragement.

Instead of fixating on high-stakes competition and flashy incentives, organizations can build a culture that values and develops the everyday contributions of the majority. Leaders can inspire lasting engagement and unlock extraordinary results by acknowledging effort, fostering a growth mindset, and creating opportunities for these employees to thrive. Recognizing and elevating good performers isn't just a "nice to have." It's the true key to long-term success.

Effort Goals Build Success, While Result Goals Chase It

You might think you're winning if you're only watching the scoreboard. After all, the runs, points, and goals are right there in big, bold numbers. But what happens when the momentum shifts, and you realize the other team isn't just playing harder—they're playing smarter? Suddenly, those numbers don't look so comforting. The pressure cranks up, stress levels spike, and before you know it, yelling becomes your go-to communication strategy. It's easy to get caught up in the score, but the truth is, the real magic isn't on the scoreboard. It's in the unseen effort. It's in the daily grind, the relentless hustle, and even the occasional coffee spill or full-blown caffeine-fueled meltdown.

When it comes to business, everyone loves a good scoreboard. However, focusing only on results is like trying to win a race by staring at the finish line instead of actually running. Numbers look great in quarterly reports, but relying too heavily on them creates a culture of shortcuts, panic, and last-minute heroics. Employees start working for the score instead of investing in their growth, and the whole operation turns into a game of high-stakes whack-a-mole. It's like judging a book by its cover or assuming someone with a full shopping cart knows how to cook. What really drives sustainable success isn't just the final score but the effort behind it. This is where understanding the difference between result goals and effort goals becomes crucial.

The result goals are the finish line. They are the quarterly revenue targets, the market share percentages, or the project deadlines. While they provide a sense of direction, they don't offer a clear roadmap on how to get there. Effort goals, on the other hand, are the day-to-day actions that fuel progress. Consistent habits, strategic planning, and relentless improvement are within our control. Consider a sales team aiming to close one million dollars in deals this quarter. If they focus only on that number, they might resort to aggressive tactics, shortcuts, or panic-driven decisions. But if they focus on effort goals, such as making a certain number of quality sales calls each week, refining their pitch, or strengthening client relationships, they naturally increase their chances of hitting the target without the chaos. The same applies to an athlete training for a marathon; instead of obsessing over finishing under four hours, they focus on logging their weekly mileage, improving their nutrition, and sticking to their training plan. In both cases, prioritizing effort makes them more likely to achieve, if not surpass, their result goals.

The truth is that focusing solely on results can be misleading and even detrimental. It can create a culture where shortcuts, quick wins, and "just get it done" attitudes reign supreme. Employees become obsessed with clicking boxes rather than improving, and before you know it, your team is burned out, disengaged, and looking for greener pastures. On the flip side, when businesses prioritize consistent hard work, continuous learning, and adaptability, they lay the groundwork for long-term success. The effort isn't flashy, but it is the foundation of every thriving company, paying off in ways the scoreboard could never capture.

Think of effort as the silent investor in your business, working behind the scenes, compounding daily, and delivering real returns over time. It is what turns average employees into top performers, small ideas into game-changing innovations, and businesses into industry leaders. Organizations can unlock greater employee engagement, higher productivity, and a healthier bottom line by shifting the focus from immediate results to sustained effort.

41

The irony is that by focusing on effort, the results take care of themselves. In short, effort over everything isn't just a catchy phrase; it's a winning business strategy.

Winning with the FOCUS Mindset

How often have you been at a sporting event and heard a coach, overly enthusiastic parent, or fan scream, "Focus!" It's the go-to word for motivation, whether it's sports, school, or business. "You just need to focus!" they shout, as if saying it louder somehow makes it easier. Next time you're at your kid's game, count how many times you hear it. Better yet, if you're coaching, try not to say it. You probably won't make it past the first quarter.

A few years ago, I made what I thought was a great life decision. I decided not to coach my youngest daughter's softball team and just enjoy being a proud, stress-free parent in the stands. You know, one of those chill parents who sit back, claps politely and resists the urge to critique every pitch. Almost immediately, I realized I had made a terrible mistake. It was like watching a slow-motion train wreck while holding a ticket I couldn't return. That season was a disaster, and not just because of the wins and losses. The endless barrage of "Focus!" screamed at the players literally gave me headaches.

Because I've spent years working with youth, high school, and college athletes, I've come to appreciate the evolution needed in coaching. The old-school, drill-sergeant style? Yeah, that doesn't fly anymore. But most coaches are former players, not trained educators. They don't always have the skill set to engage young athletes in a productive and emotionally supportive way. They think the end goal is winning that under-10 (u10) recreation championship. When in reality, it's about giving kids a life experience they'll carry with them forever, whether it's a confidence boost or, unfortunately, an emotional scar that could last longer than their playing career.

Back to the "F" word. The coach loved that word. He screamed it more than a toddler discovering their first favorite word. Every play, every error, every missed opportunity… "Focus!" And the parents? They joined in like a choir, echoing the same thing from the bleachers. I couldn't help but wonder. What exactly do they think the kids are doing out there? Daydreaming about snacks? Probably. But that's not the point. The real issue was this: Nobody actually taught them what focusing meant.

By the time playoffs rolled around, "focus" was every other word out of the coach's mouth. Our family had heard it so much it officially became a bad word in our house. Now, when someone says "focus," we give them a look and respond, "Watch your language!" It's been permanently rebranded as the "F" word. And let's just say it has replaced what you originally thought of when you read that phrase. That's how bad it got.

The problem is that no one actually explains what focusing looks like in sports or business. Whenever I work with coaches or business professionals, I love to challenge them: "Explain to me how to focus." Cue the awkward silence and blank stares. Then I make it easier: "Okay, show me how to focus." That's when the real struggle begins. If we can't explain or demonstrate focus ourselves, how can we expect athletes, employees, or managers to figure it out on their own?

Since it's highly unlikely that the "F" word isn't going anywhere in the business world, maybe it's time we redefine it. Instead of using it as an empty buzzword, we need to start providing real context by teaching people how actually to focus on their work. In the pursuit of success, it's easy to get distracted by things beyond our control. Market trends, competition, office politics, or even whether it's going to rain on the day of a big presentation can impact our goals. But true progress and mastery come from honing in on what can be controlled. That's where the Focus Mindset comes in. This simple yet powerful approach helps individuals and leaders direct their energy toward what truly matters, fostering a sense of ownership, resilience, and sustainable success. Another key step in the 90% advantage.

F – Find What You Can Control

The first step in mastering control is finding out what is within your control because nearly everything is simply out of your hands. Effort, attitude, and how you respond to challenges? Those are all yours to manage. But the competition's next move? The economy's wild rollercoaster ride? Your coworker's obsession with using "synergy" in every meeting? Yeah, not so much. The problem is that too many people waste valuable time and mental energy stressing over things they cannot change, like refreshing their email inbox every 30 seconds or trying to predict next quarter's market trends with the accuracy of a weather forecast.

Here's where we can all take a page from the Serenity Prayer playbook—because, yes, it applies to business just as much as it does to life. The message is simple but gold: focus on what you can control, let go of what you can't, and learn how to know the difference. That wisdom isn't just a nice idea in today's fast-paced, unpredictable world of ever-changing market conditions and never-ending competition. It's survival. Success comes from accepting the uncertainties while doubling down on areas where you do have influence, like your effort, strategy, and leadership.

So, instead of obsessing over things you cannot control (like whether the Wi-Fi will hold up during your big presentation), shift your focus to what you can like your preparation, your adaptability, and your relentless commitment to improvement. Because when you channel your energy into the right places, meaningful progress happens, and suddenly, those external distractions no longer seem so overwhelming.

O – Own Your Actions

Once you've figured out what's within your control, the next step is taking full ownership of your actions because nobody else will do it for you. This means being accountable for your decisions, your work ethic, and even that not-so-great idea you pitched in last week's meeting. No excuses. No blame games. No pointing fingers at Janet from accounting because the numbers didn't magically add up. Leaders who truly own it create an environment where effort and progress thrive.

Plenty of people can talk the talk. They say the right words and the perfect soundbites and always seem to nail it in meetings with just the right amount of corporate buzzwords. And then there are those who can walk the walk. They definitely look the part. Their actions scream leadership, and they know how to command attention with their presence. But when leaders walk the talk, it's a game-changer. It's not just about saying the right things or looking the part. It is about showing up consistently, following through, and proving with actions that accountability isn't just a concept. It's a way of operating.

When a leader walks the talk, it creates a ripple effect. Teams don't just hear about accountability. They see it, they feel it, and before long, they start living it. It's like positivity but with real impact. Employees become more engaged, motivated, and inspired to take ownership of their own work because they know they're part of a culture where accountability isn't just lip service. It's the standard. And the best part? It becomes contagious in the most productive way, spreading across teams faster than office gossip (but with way better results).

Owning your actions isn't just a feel-good leadership mantra. It builds confidence and earns credibility both inside and outside the organization. When people know you're someone who takes responsibility—whether things go right or wrong—it fosters trust, encourages innovation, and sets the stage for continuous improvement. Nothing feels better than knowing you're in control of your success, except maybe leaving work early on a Friday. But by then, you've earned it!

C – Consistency Creates Champions

Consistency is the not-so-secret ingredient to sustained effort and long-term success. It's not about those occasional bursts of motivation. Like when you suddenly decide to organize your entire inbox at 3 a.m. or hit the gym after watching one inspiring YouTube video. No, real success comes from showing up every single day. No excuses.

Consistency is what separates the pros from the amateurs. It builds momentum, strengthens habits, and saves you from the "I'll start fresh on Monday" trap. Think of it like brushing your teeth: doing it once really well won't cut it, but doing it every day keeps cavities from forming.

Consistency does not mean perfection It means persistence. It's about making steady progress, learning from mistakes, and staying committed to the process even when results aren't immediate. So, remember that success isn't built in a day, whether you're tackling a major project, training for a marathon, or just trying to drink more water (because hydration is hard). It's built daily.

U – Understand the Process

Success doesn't happen instantly. No matter how much we all wish it were. It's not like ordering fast food where you expect immediate gratification. Instead, success is more like a slow cooker. It requires time, patience, and the right ingredients mixed in consistently to get the best results. Understanding that small, deliberate actions, repeated over time, are what lead to those big wins helps individuals stay the course, even when progress feels about as fast as molasses in January.

Sticking with the process can be tough, especially when results don't come flying in as fast as a you'd like. But embracing the journey fosters patience, persistence, and a long-term commitment to growth. It's about showing up, doing the work, and trusting that all those small wins will eventually add up.

The best leaders understand that effort compounds over time, like interest in a well-managed savings account.

Instead of money, you're investing in skills, resilience, and progress. They encourage their teams to focus on continuous improvement rather than chasing instant gratification. Shortcuts rarely lead anywhere great. You might get lucky cutting corners once, but in the long run, it's those who stay consistent, stay committed, and keep grinding, even when things get tough, who come out on top.

S – Stay Resilient

Resilience is the duct tape that holds everything together when things start falling apart at the seams. No matter how much effort you put in, setbacks are inevitable. Projects will flop, plans will unravel, and sometimes, it will feel like everything is on fire (including your inbox). But the people who truly succeed are not the ones who never fail. They are the ones who fail, fix, and forge ahead with even more determination than before.

We'll dive deeper into the beautiful mess that is learning from mistakes in the next chapter, but for now, let's get one thing straight: mistakes are not the enemy. In fact, they're your greatest (albeit sometimes embarrassing) teachers. They provide valuable lessons, much like touching a hot stove teaches you that, yes, it really is hot. Pain is a great educator. You don't need to learn that lesson a second time. Resilient individuals don't let setbacks define them. Instead, they treat failures like learning opportunities rather than stumbling blocks. Tripping over them isn't fun, but getting back up makes all the difference.

One of my favorite questions to ask an audience is this: "If you had to choose, would you rather ride the merry-go-round or the roller coaster?" The answer is usually pretty telling and sets the stage for what comes next.

The merry-go-round lovers are all about the safe and predictable experience. No surprises, no sudden jolt. Just a smooth ride with the wind in your hair, the gentle up-and-down of a composite horse, and the comforting sounds of calliope music playing in the background. It's consistent, it's reliable, and let's be honest, it's not exactly going to spike your adrenaline. Sure, it's enjoyable, but it's also the same thing over and over.

Then, there are the roller coaster fans. The thrill-seekers, the adrenaline junkies, the ones who live for the unexpected. They love the towering climbs, the stomach-dropping falls, and the sheer exhilaration of not knowing what's around the next bend. The loops, the twists, and the breakneck speed are all part of the fun. They embrace the unpredictability and know that the most exciting parts of the ride come from the unexpected turns and the rush that follows.

Here's the reality: life is a roller coaster. Sure, there are moments that feel like a merry-go-round—safe, steady, and routine. But for the most part, life, work, and business are anything but predictable. They're full of highs and lows, slow climbs, sudden drops, and unexpected loops that leave you questioning your sanity. And let's face it the roller coaster is a heck of a lot more fun.

If you're someone who prefers the steady, predictable rhythm of the merry-go-round, it's no surprise that work can feel overwhelming when it suddenly throws you for a loop. Constant change, uncertainty, and unexpected challenges can leave you feeling stuck, frustrated, and maybe even a little motion-sick. But life, like work, isn't designed to move in perfect circles. It's a roller coaster, full of ups and downs, sharp turns, and the occasional heart-stopping drop. The sooner you learn to lean into the ride, embrace the chaos, and enjoy the thrill of the unexpected, the sooner you realize that those challenges aren't roadblocks. They are part of the adventure. And the best part? No matter how wild the ride gets, it always moves forward.

Once you understand your ride preference and build resilience, adopting a solution-focused mindset is the key to navigating the inevitable twists and turns. Think of yourself as part detective—always looking for clues and solutions—part problem-solver, and just a little bit of an optimist. Instead of getting stuck replaying what went wrong, resilient people shift gears. They channel their energy into finding ways to make things right, adjusting their approach, and returning stronger next time. They understand that success is rarely a straight shot to the top. It is more like a squiggly, looping, occasionally backtracking roller coaster. And that's a good thing. Because, unlike the predictable, safe merry-go-round, the roller coaster is where real growth, excitement, and progress happen.

Applying FOCUS

The FOCUS Mindset isn't just a strategy in a world that's constantly changing and throwing unexpected challenges our way. It's a survival skill. It's about shifting your energy away from the things that are not in your control and directing it toward what truly matters: your effort, your attitude, and your response to the roller coaster of life and work. By embracing FOCUS, you cultivate the discipline to stay on track, the ownership to take responsibility, the consistency to keep moving forward, the understanding to trust the process, and the resilience to bounce back stronger after setbacks.

Life isn't a smooth, predictable merry-go-round. It's a wild, unpredictable roller coaster filled with highs, lows, and unexpected twists. But with the FOCUS Mindset, you're not just along for the ride. You're in the driver's seat, ready to tackle every challenge with clarity and confidence. Whether you're leading a team, building a business, or just trying to navigate the chaos of daily life, FOCUS gives you the tools to stay grounded, adaptable, and, most importantly, keep moving forward.

This is where the 90% advantage takes shape. Success isn't built on a single big win but on a series of small, consistent actions taken by everyday contributors. The employees who quietly keep the organization running. By maintaining FOCUS, you can guide these efforts toward meaningful, long-term success, helping individuals and teams rise to new levels of performance. It's about recognizing that the path to greatness lies not in dramatic, fleeting moments of victory but in the steady, incremental growth that compounds over time.

> *"Life isn't a smooth, predictable merry-go-round. It's a wild, unpredictable roller coaster filled with highs, lows, and unexpected twists."*

So, breathe deep, embrace the ups and downs, and remember that success isn't about avoiding the ride. It's about learning to enjoy it, one intentional step at a time. Stay FOCUSed, stay committed, and watch how the small, consistent efforts—your *90% advantage*—lead to the big, meaningful results you've been striving for.

As you may recall, we jokingly refer to FOCUS as the "f-word" in our family. It's tossed around in meetings, slapped on PowerPoint slides, and overused to the point of eye rolls. But now, hopefully, you see it differently. This particular "f-word" isn't about pressure. It's about purpose. It's a mindset, a guide, a way to cut through the noise and keep moving toward what matters most.

The next time someone tells you to FOCUS, lean in, lock in, and lead with intention. It is how effort becomes impact. It is how progress takes root. And when you live it, lead it, and model it, you build better results and help others find their direction, too. That's the real power of the 90% advantage.

GOOGLE – HOW FOCUSING ON EFFORT TRANSFORMED ITS WORKFORCE

Google, one of the world's most influential technology companies, has long been known for its innovative culture and dynamic work environment. However, what truly sets Google apart is its strategic focus on effort. A belief that hard work, persistence, and continuous improvement are the keys to long-term success. Google has built a culture that recognizes and rewards effort, leading to remarkable outcomes in employee engagement, innovation, and sustained business growth. As the company rapidly expanded, Google's leadership understood that fostering effort-based values, encouraging employees to take initiative, embrace challenges, and learn from failure would be critical to sustaining its competitive edge and driving long-term success.

Using an effort-driven culture, Google implemented several key strategies that reinforced effort as a core value:

1. **Encouraging Employee Engagement:** Employees were encouraged to pursue ideas outside their immediate job scope, fostering a culture of ownership, creativity, and motivation. As a result, employee satisfaction and engagement levels soared, with many employees citing a deep sense of purpose and autonomy in their roles.

2. **Fostering Innovation Through Effort:** Employees were encouraged to experiment, take calculated

risks, and view failures as learning opportunities rather than setbacks. This mindset led to the creation of groundbreaking products such as Gmail, Google Maps, and Google Photos.

3. **Driving Business Growth:** Employees who feel valued for their contributions are more likely to stay committed, resulting in lower turnover rates and a more resilient organization.

Google's emphasis on effort has produced remarkable results across multiple organizational dimensions. By fostering a culture that values hard work and persistence, the company significantly reduced employee turnover, as individuals who felt valued and empowered were more likely to stay, resulting in lower attrition rates and a more committed workforce. Google's experience demonstrates that when organizations cultivate an environment where effort is recognized and rewarded, they unlock their workforce's full potential. The company's journey serves as a compelling example for businesses seeking to build a growth-oriented culture. One where effort is not just encouraged but celebrated as the cornerstone of innovation and long-term success.

COACHING FOR EFFORT
OVER OUTCOME

Here are five strategies to help leaders emphasize effort, resilience, and sustainable performance:

1. **Prioritize effort goals**. Redefine success by focusing less on final outcomes and more on the daily actions that drive them. Guide your team to set effort-based goals like "number of client touchpoints" or "skill development benchmarks." These create a culture of progress and consistency.

2. **Celebrate consistency**. Recognize team members who show up, stay committed, and build steady momentum. Highlighting reliable performers reinforces that grit and discipline matter just as much as flash and speed.

3. **Name the scoreboard mentality.** Talk openly about the trap of obsessing over results. When leaders name it, they tame it—shifting focus back to learning, growth, and long-term strategy instead of short-term wins.

4. **Model resilience in the roller coaster.** When things go sideways, don't just fix the issue—share how you're navigating the setback. Let your team see how leaders bounce back, recalibrate, and stay on course.

5. **Make FOCUS part of your feedback.** Use the FO-

CUS framework as a structure for coaching conversations. It's not just a mindset—it's a practical lens for navigating effort, growth, and setbacks.

Effort isn't about trying harder—it's about being smarter, consistently. Leaders who champion effort over ego, growth over glory, and persistence over perfection build teams that outperform the scoreboard every time.

"I believe in the sweet spot."

— Crash Davis in Bull Durham

3.

Engaging The Bench Player

Things were falling into place at the beginning of my under-12 summer baseball season. After a year spent in the shadows of the bench, I was finally named the starting second baseman. A role I cherished with every step I took onto the field. The bond I shared with my long-time friends, who were also my teammates, made the achievement feel even more significant. For a moment, life was perfect.

But as the saying goes, the game humbles you, and mine came swiftly. Just a few games in, my once-promising fielding ability unraveled before my eyes. In the first inning, a routine ground ball rolled toward me—an easy play, or so I thought. Instead, the ball slipped through my legs. By the third inning, it happened again. Another ground ball, but this time, it ricocheted off my foot and slowly rolled toward the right-field line. The worst was yet to come. In the next inning, I fumbled another simple play, and with it, I handed the opposing team two runs and a crushing loss.

I was devastated. My coach, a man of few words, chose this moment to become a man of no words. As the team gathered in left field after the game, he spoke briefly to everyone, offering generic words of encouragement but not a single glance or acknowledgment toward me. His silence was suffocating.

From that moment forward, everything changed. I didn't just lose my spot as a starter—I was erased. Practices became an exercise in self-doubt, and games felt like endless stretches of wondering if I was even part of the team anymore. No longer a starter, backup, or even the guy who hands out water bottles, I was relegated to the bench, an outcast in my own mind. Once burning with the intensity of a fastball, my passion for the game began to flicker and fade. Like a ball foul-tipped into the catcher's mitt. That summer, I didn't just learn about the bench's punishment. I became intimately acquainted with it, earning my PhD in its cold, unyielding reality.

That memory became a defining moment in my life and throughout my career. I worked tirelessly to avoid being a bench player. The stress, anxiety, and emotional toll I placed on myself lingered for nearly two decades. Maybe you participated in sports, band, theater, or another extra-curricular activity that pushed you to excel. If so, you might think, "That's a good thing—those life lessons shaped me, motivating me to strive for my best." And you'd be right. I recognize that the fear of failure and the thought of sitting on the sidelines drove me to become better, stronger, and more efficient. But it also made me an overachiever, constantly anxious about making mistakes, and left me dreading the lump in my throat whenever my supervisor asked to talk.

When speaking with athletes, coaches, or parents, I always make time to share this story. It highlights how some coaches use punishment—or even the mere threat of it—as their go-to strategy to motivate players as if fear and dread were part of the game plan. It also delves into the uncomfortable reality of parents shelling out thousands of dollars for their child's sports, hoping their investment translates into more touches, innings, or minutes on the field. (Because, let's be honest, nothing says "return on investment," like a under-10 player getting five extra minutes of playing time in a weekend tournament.)

The message becomes painfully obvious: The bench is seen as a bad place—a purgatory for the weakest players. It fosters a relentless fear of failure and mistakes, branding players with an invisible scarlet letter that whispers, "You're not good enough" every time they sit down.

No matter your position in the professional hierarchy, you will likely find yourself managing people at some point. Leadership styles are often shaped by learned behavior. Drawn from the managers who came before us, the executives we admired, and the coaches we encountered in our athletic experiences. These influences form the foundation of how we perceive and handle mistakes and failures, whether we accept them as growth opportunities or see them as insurmountable flaws.

> *"Bench players aren't just placeholders...*
> *Recognition and success do not belong solely to*
> *the stars who score the points but also to those*
> *who make those opportunities possible."*

In the workplace, groups of people are often referred to as teams. This terminology tends to bring back memories of past team experiences, whether it's from childhood soccer leagues or navigating your current corporate world. Interestingly, in most workplaces, teams are typically led by managers or supervisors—not exactly the "coach" archetype you'd expect. (Let's face it: very few managers are out there shouting motivational speeches like a football coach at halftime.) Even in professional sports, most teams have a head coach—except for baseball, where the leader is a manager, perhaps because it's the one sport where chewing gum and spitting sunflower seeds qualify as a job skill.

Whether or not you've played sports, the business world is overflowing with metaphors and examples drawn from athletics, many of which will surface throughout this book. You'll be encouraged to reflect on the best coaches, teachers, and managers who left a lasting positive impact on you. And yes, you'll also revisit those individuals whose words—or actions—left you cringing, questioning, or plotting an early retirement.

But here's the truth. A truth that also emphasizes the 90% advantage. Bench players aren't just placeholders. Think of the movie Rudy. They are crucial to a team's success. These overlooked players often serve as the scout team in sports, simulating opponents to help starters prepare for the next big game. They push the starters to stay sharp, ready to step in when needed, and keep the team moving forward behind the scenes. Recognition and success do not belong solely to the stars who score the points but also to those who make those opportunities possible. The same is true in business.

Every workplace has its "high potential" superstars. They fill the highlight reels, land the big deals, or deliver the show-stopping presentations. They are the go-to people when stakes are high, the first ones considered for promotions, and often the faces of an organization's success. But as impressive as they are, organizations do not run on superstars alone. Success isn't just about the top players but the entire team. And in every team, there are bench players. The overlooked, underutilized employees with untapped potential waiting to be unlocked.

Just like great coaches understand the importance of depth in their rosters, great leaders recognize that an organization's strength lies in its top performers and the entire team. These everyday contributors can become extraordinary assets with the right mindset and strategies. By investing in their development, fostering intrinsic motivation, and providing opportunities for growth, leaders unlock the full capacity of their teams. This is the core of The 90% Advantage. Empowering the quiet majority to rise, thrive, and help carry the organization to greater success.

These individuals may not be the ones you call upon to save the day in a crisis, at least not yet. But with the right support and recognition, they become the steady force that sustains progress. Organizations that embrace this approach discover that their success isn't about any single star player. It's about the depth, resilience, and dedication of the entire team working together to win.

Uncovering Hidden Potential

Every team has its stars. Those who rack up points, make headlines, and bask in the glory of the spotlight. But ask any seasoned coach, and they'll tell you that championships aren't won on star power alone. The field goals, the often-overlooked, steady contributions quietly determine victory. The same is true in the workplace. Hidden among your ranks are the "benchwarmers" of your team. Employees who may not seek attention but whose consistent efforts and untapped potential are crucial to long-term success. They aren't the loudest voices or the first to volunteer, but these hidden talents can become your organization's secret weapon with the right strategies. The key is learning how to recognize, engage, and develop them before the scoreboard reminds you just how much those three-point plays matter.

Uncovering hidden potential is an art that separates good managers from great leaders. It's easy to focus on the top performers. The equivalent of your star quarterback or ace pitcher. But the real strength of any team lies deeper in the roster. Your benchwarmers are those employees who quietly handle the routine tasks, keep things moving behind the scenes, and never clamor for praise. They may not stand out at first glance, but when the stakes are high and you need a clutch performance, these are the people who can step up and make a difference. Yet, if left overlooked, their potential may go untapped indefinitely. So, how do you bring these everyday heroes into the game meaningfully? The answer lies in recognizing the moments when they shine in small but impactful ways and giving them opportunities to develop further. The following strategies offer a playbook to help you identify, engage, and elevate these hidden contributors, turning them into your organization's field goal specialists. Small, consistent wins that add up to big success.

Research has shown that employees crave four fundamental things: to be heard, seen, safe, and valued. And when employees speak up to share ideas or insights, nothing deflates their motivation faster than being shut down, especially in front of their peers. Sure, most people can tolerate a bit of rejection behind closed doors, but public humiliation? That sticks. The sting of being dismissed can push employees to retreat into "do the bare minimum" mode, leaving them disengaged and unwilling to take further risks. That's not exactly the formula for innovation.

Being heard is just the beginning. Employees also want to be seen as unique contributors with valuable skills and potential. Everybody comes with a mix of strengths and weaknesses, but a manager with a coach's mindset can help employees play to their strengths while guiding them to improve in areas that need growth. This approach fosters a sense of purpose and builds trust, which in turn helps employees unlock their full potential.

Of course, it's not just about growth opportunities. We live in times that feel like a never-ending disaster movie montage. Social media and news outlets constantly scream about doomsday scenarios, the job market can pivot on a dime, and the cost of simply keeping up with everyday life seems to climb higher by the week. For anyone outside the one percent, navigating day-to-day financial uncertainty is like riding an emotional roller coaster without a seatbelt. Franklin D. Roosevelt famously said in his first inaugural address, "The only thing we have to fear is fear itself." FDR didn't have Instagram, a stock portfolio, or anxiety when filling up a gas tank after seeing last week's prices. Fear is everywhere. In the workplace, at home, and everywhere in between.

This is why a safe work environment, both physically and mentally, is non-negotiable. Employees need to know they can bring their full selves to work without fear of being judged, dismissed, or blindsided by an emotional ambush from a passive-aggressive coworker or boss. Safety isn't just about fire drills; it's about fostering emotional well-being and psychological security so employees feel empowered to engage fully with their work.

> *"Being heard is just the beginning. Employees also want to be seen as unique contributors with valuable skills and potential."*

Now, let's talk about Zillennials (that delightful mix of Gen Z and late Millennials) entering the workforce. These are the digital natives who've spent their formative years marinating in Wi-Fi and viral memes. Their expectations for work-life balance and respect are...let's say, different. Remember the "pay your dues" mentality that once defined career advancement? Yeah, no. That's as appealing to them as dial-up internet. This generation expects to be valued from day one and is not shy about it. They want their ideas recognized without a manager saying, "Well, back in my day..." Because, frankly, they weren't around for your day. A smart leader knows that valuing their contribution early builds loyalty and engagement and keeps you from becoming the next viral "Boomer Manager Fails" meme.

And if you think they're going to stick around out of loyalty alone, think again. Millennials and Zillennials are changing jobs more often than previous generations. Studies show the average young professional today changes roles every two to three years. Sometimes, even sooner if the culture doesn't click or the growth path feels stale. It's not flakiness. It is a strategy. They're not afraid to pivot, explore, and find a place where their contributions are valued and their well-being isn't considered a "perk." That means retaining them isn't about locking them in. It's about giving them a reason to stay.

By cultivating a workplace where employees, whether seasoned benchwarmers or eager staff, feel seen, heard, and safe, you create a culture where the potential is nurtured and success is sustained. After all, people perform their best when they believe the coach is rooting for them, not sidelining their dreams.

The bench players don't need to stay on the sidelines forever. A great coach ensures all players get into the game. Maybe the star player is exhausted, injured, or just plain stuck in a slump. When that benchwarmer steps onto the field, their performance can make or break the game. But whether they rise to the occasion or trip over their own shoelaces depends on how well-prepared they are. Have they been given opportunities to practice under pressure, or were they just asked to fetch water and warm the bench?

In the workplace, the same dynamic applies. You never know when one of your top performers might be out of commission, burned, or have a family emergency, or maybe they've finally used all their PTO to explore every national park. When that moment comes, you'll need someone to step in and carry the team. But if your hidden talent has never been challenged beyond their day-to-day tasks, they'll be as overwhelmed as a substitute teacher facing a classroom full of caffeinated teens.

Take Jane from Marketing as an example. She's reliable, quiet, and methodical. She is great with numbers but always stays in her lane. One day, your company's lead financial analyst calls in sick two hours before a major client meeting. Cue the panic. Instead of scrambling, you call on Jane. Why? Last quarter, you assigned her to lead a cross-functional budget-planning project. It stretched her beyond her comfort zone, but she gained confidence in presenting her work to different teams and solving high-pressure problems. Now, when she steps into that client meeting, she's ready. Not only does Jane nail the presentation, but she also improvises a brilliant solution on the spot, earning a round of applause. By the time your financial analyst returns, Jane is already receiving kudos and maybe even scouting for her next challenge.

Now ask yourself this: Who is your next Jane? If one of your trusted stars had to step away tomorrow, which team member would be ready and willing to step in and deliver? That answer doesn't come from chance; it comes from leadership. It comes from how intentionally you develop the people who aren't always in the spotlight. The truth is that every team has hidden talent. The question is whether you're cultivating it or letting it go unnoticed. Great leaders don't just build stars. They build depth. Because when the pressure is on, it's not about who shines the brightest. It's about who is ready.

This is the 90% advantage: recognizing that your so-called benchwarmers are often your best insurance policy against the unexpected when given opportunities to grow and develop. They're your adaptable, resilient players who can rise to any challenge, and if you've invested in them early, they won't just step up. They'll shine. So, go ahead. Assign that "*extra*" project. You might just discover you've got a few all-stars waiting in the wings.

The beauty of the bench is that it provides the best seat in the house. From there, players get a bird's-eye view of everything. Who's making smart plays, who's falling apart under pressure, and who's the glue keeping the team together when the chips are down? It's no different in the workplace. While leaders are often too busy focusing on the high-profile players (or fighting fires), the people on the "bench" have a front-row seat to the real MVPs: the quiet contributors who step up when no one's watching, solve problems without drama and rally the team when morale takes a nosedive.

Here we have Marcus. He isn't flashy. He's not the one raising his hand at every meeting with a "brilliant" idea or sending 12-paragraph emails full of corporate buzzwords. But when tension is high, Marcus is the one who keeps his cool while everyone else is spinning. Like when the IT system crashes ten minutes before a client pitch, he is the guy who calmly says, "Let me make a few calls," and somehow, magically, everything is back online within five minutes. His coworkers know that Marcus is the one to go to when disaster strikes or when someone needs level-headed advice. But without a formal recognition system, leadership would never know that Marcus is basically the workplace equivalent of a Swiss Army knife.

That's why a peer recognition program is so powerful. Instead of waiting for managers to notice the unsung heroes, it allows colleagues to call out the quiet MVPs. Over time, patterns emerge. You start seeing the same names popping up in shout-outs: the person who saved the day with quick thinking, the one who always steps up to mentor new hires, or the behind-the-scenes problem-solver who keeps projects on track.

These are your field goal specialists. The steady, consistent contributors who may not seek glory but add crucial points to the scoreboard. In the heat of the moment, when all eyes are on the star players, these are the people who quietly clinch the win. Recognizing and developing them gives your team a *90% Advantage* because it elevates those everyday contributions that often go unnoticed but are essential to your organization's success. So next time Marcus works his magic, don't just say "Thanks." Give him that peer-nominated "Silent Hero Award" (and maybe a coffee on the house). He's earned it.

When was the last time you really dug into your bench-warmers' résumés? I'm not talking about the quick skim you did when they applied three years ago. I mean, really looked. You might be in for some surprises. Maybe that quiet data analyst with a talent for creating pivot tables also has a psychology degree and could help with employee engagement. Or perhaps your steady HR coordinator, who you thought spent weekends binge-watching crime dramas, is actually a certified leadership coach who spends Saturdays running workshops at the local community center. People are full of hidden talents. The problem is that most of us never bother to ask.

Maybe you have Debbie, known around the office as the queen of spreadsheets. If Excel were a kingdom, she'd have a throne built entirely from color-coded tabs. One day, during a casual chat at the coffee machine, her manager asked, "So, what do you do outside of work?" Debbie had spent ten years as a professional event planner before switching careers. By the end of the week, Debbie was spearheading the company's next annual conference, negotiating better contracts with vendors than anyone thought possible. Suddenly, she was no longer just "the spreadsheet queen" but "Debbie the Deal Closer."

Or there's Roger, the IT support guy who everyone assumed lived in a basement filled with blinking servers. When his manager finally sat down for a talent audit, they discovered that Roger moonlighted as a stand-up comedian. His knack for storytelling and humor became a game-changer in team meetings. He went from fixing printers to leading creative brainstorming sessions because nothing sparks ideas like someone who can get the room laughing. Roger is now the go-to guy for client pitches because he knows how to captivate a crowd and make even technical jargon sound exciting.

These conversations aren't just small talk but windows into untapped potential. Just like discovering that your veteran bench player can play multiple positions, exploring employees' hidden talents lets you reposition them in ways that benefit both their growth and the organization's goals. This isn't just a feel-good strategy; it's a *90% advantage* in action. People thrive when they're aligned with roles that engage their full skill set. So, take some time to sit down with your team members. You never know. You might find out your office assistant has a secret talent for project management or that your marketing intern once ran a successful TikTok brand. If you don't ask, you'll never know.

Here's an expression I'm sure you've heard: "When the cats are away, the mice will play." But sometimes, when the cats are away, the mice actually get to work. They start offering insights and solutions that never make it into formal meetings but are often the most practical and innovative ideas in the room. There are moments when staff feel comfortable with each other in your absence, letting down their guard and sharing what's really on their minds. Benchwarmers often give the best advice when the coach isn't hovering over them. They see things the coach might miss because they're observing from the sidelines, where they have time to think without the pressure of making split-second decisions. The same dynamic plays out in the workplace. Your hidden gems often shine in those un-scripted, informal moments, like a casual chat by the coffee machine, a quick hallway conversation, or a snack room debate over whether pineapple belongs on pizza.

Take Mike from Ops. He's the guy who rarely speaks up in meetings but can fix just about anything. One morn-ing, over a coffee machine that had mysteriously decided it only brews decaf (which everyone agreed was a crisis of epic proportions), Mike casually mentioned a new software integration that could streamline inventory management. His manager, who happened to be within earshot, perked up faster than someone who finally found a hidden stash of real coffee. That small comment led to a major overhaul in operations that saved the company thousands. If the manager hadn't been paying attention, they'd have missed a game-changing play.

These moments are golden because they're pressure-free. People aren't worried about impressing the boss or hit-ting a deadline. They're just being themselves. And in that relaxed state, real problem-solving and leadership abilities often emerge. You might notice that Susan from Marketing is the one who naturally de-escalates office drama by crack-ing a well-timed joke or that Jake is the one who quietly gets everyone aligned on priorities without any formal authority. These are your hidden gems. Employees who, with a bit of encouragement and opportunity, can turn those informal moments of brilliance into major contributions.

This is the 90% advantage. Finding unexpected talent and innovation in everyday situations. The trick is to be present and listen. Don't just zone out in the break room while checking your phone. Be curious. Ask questions. You never know who might have the next great idea. Maybe even the quiet guy who just fixed the coffee machine. (At the very least, he's earned a promotion to "office hero.")

Supporting Bench Players Elevates the Whole Team

I love sports movies. They're my go-to genre. Whether it's an inspiring drama like Miracle, where the underdog 1980 U.S. hockey team defeated the seemingly invincible Soviets to win Olympic gold, giving us Al Michaels's legendary call, "Do you believe in miracles?" Or a powerful story of triumph over adversity like Remember the Titans. In that film, a racially divided town is forced to confront its prejudices when a Black coach takes over the high school football team. The tension builds to a pivotal playoff moment when the former coach (now assistant) calls out the corrupt officiating and fires up the defense with an unforgettable line: "I don't want them to gain another yard!"

And then there's Bull Durham, a comedy classic that gives us an inside peek at the grind of minor league baseball. Players ride buses from one small-town ballpark to the next, chasing their dreams of making it to the big leagues. In one hilarious scene, the exasperated coach storms into the locker room, shoves his team into the showers, and be-rates them for being "lollygaggers." I still don't know exact-ly what a lollygagger is, but it sure makes for a great laugh!

There are hundreds of sports movies that provide powerful insights, entertainment, and inspiration for the workplace. They're filled with lessons and parallels that re-flect real-life challenges, ambitions, and achievements. At the core of many of these stories is the concept of culture. Sometimes, it's a culture in desperate need of change—one that's holding people back. Other times, it's a culture that needs small tweaks to unlock the potential for success. And occasionally, it's a culture so toxic that it feels impossible to survive—until one person, or a team, rises against the odds and finds a way to push through.

Not every sports story ends with a victory parade or a championship trophy. But in both sports and life, when a significant cultural shift takes place—when people evolve, support one another, and strive for something greater—it's not just the final score that matters. It's the transformation along the way that leaves a lasting impact.

In the workplace, the same principle applies. One per-son might lead a project, but the data analyst who prepared the reports, the IT tech who fixed the system crash at 2 a.m., and the admin assistant who triple-checked the pres-entation slides all contributed to that success. When these behind-the-scenes players feel valued, they stay engaged, motivated, and ready to perform the next time the pressure is on.

Who is responsible for the culture in your department, section, office, and workplace? The answer is simple: you. Leaders who engage all employees, especially the so-called "bench players," and build a culture that includes everyone, not just the top performers, often see remarkable results. People respond positively when they feel valued and part of something greater.

As mentioned before, human beings crave purpose, a sense of belonging, and someone who believes in them. But it doesn't stop there. Employees also want to enjoy their work, build meaningful friendships, and thrive in a positive, competitive environment. This doesn't mean everyone gets a trophy. It means that everyone is given a fair shot at success—regardless of age, experience, or any other characteristic. When that kind of culture takes root, teams win on and off the field.

> *"Employees also want to enjoy their work, build meaningful friendships, and thrive in a positive, competitive environment."*

Creating a culture that celebrates these contributions can be both strategic and fun. Imagine starting a "Shadow MVP" award program that recognizes the people whose work often goes unnoticed but is crucial to the organization's success. You might be surprised to find that some of your biggest victories are being held together by someone who knows how to fast-track orders during supply chain meltdowns, someone who intuitively adjusts the office temperature to avoid "thermostat wars" that could lead to a mutiny.

Another opportunity is to use humor and creativity in recognizing contributions. Implement a "Game Tape Playback" session during all-hands meetings, where you share funny and memorable highlights of the month's achievements, giving shoutouts to those who saved the day in unexpected ways. For example, imagine a staff member being hailed as the office hero for organizing an impromptu "umbrella relay" to escort coworkers to their cars during a surprise downpour. The simple act of turning a rainy disaster into a fun, team-building event not only boosts morale but also strengthens the sense of camaraderie. It's these moments of humor and collaboration that remind everyone that success is built together—every role and every effort matters.

Supporting bench players also means giving them opportunities to grow. Leaders can assign stretch projects, provide mentorship, or rotate employees through different roles to expand their skills. You never know. There might be that one person who always seemed content fixing printers has a talent for process innovation that can save your company thousands. Encouraging these employees to step into the spotlight occasionally isn't about replacing your star players; it's about ensuring you have depth, resilience, and a culture where everyone thrives.

Ultimately, when bench players feel seen and supported, they become champions of the culture itself. They inspire others by showing that recognition isn't reserved for those in the limelight. And when everyone feels invested in the team's success, collective achievement becomes not just a goal but a way of life. After all, field goals may not get the crowd roaring, but they add up fast—and before you know it, you've quietly secured the win.

PLANET FITNESS – A WINNING STRATEGY BUILT ON INCLUSION, EMPOWERMENT, AND CONSISTENT GROWTH

Planet Fitness has redefined success in the fitness industry by focusing on a demographic most gyms had long ignored: the 90% of people who want to get healthier but
feel intimidated by traditional gym culture. Unlike facilities
designed for elite athletes, where six-pack abs, slamming
weights, and unsolicited flexing in mirrors are the norm,
Planet Fitness built a brand centered on safety, belonging,
and steady progress. Their "No Judgment Zone" philosophy reflects three key pillars: a healthy culture, a commitment to serving the everyday members and empowering
individuals to achieve continuous growth.

1. **A Healthy Culture: Eliminating Intimidation and
   Judgment** – Planet Fitness knew that the average
   person walking into a gym didn't want to compete
   with bodybuilders or be surrounded by "lunks"
   (their term for weight-slamming gym bros). Many
   people are already anxious when they start a fitness
   journey, and traditional gyms often amplify that
   anxiety with an overwhelming atmosphere. Planet
   Fitness took a radically different approach, creating
   a "No Judgment Zone" designed to reduce intimidation and make everyone feel welcome. To enforce
   this culture, they introduced the now-famous Lunk

Alarm, a literal alarm that sounds if someone drops weights dramatically or engages in intimidating behavior. Trainers and staff are encouraged to create a positive, approachable environment where members can exercise without fear of judgment. Whether it's a first-timer nervous about stepping onto a treadmill or a veteran maintaining their routine, everyone is treated with the same respect and encouragement.

2. **Focusing on the 90%: Serving the Everyday Member –** Most gyms cater to the top 10%—the fitness fanatics who thrive in high-intensity environments. The problem? That leaves the majority of people feeling alienated. Planet Fitness recognized that these "everyday exercisers" were an untapped market. Most people just want to stay healthy, lose a little weight, or feel good in their bodies without having to train like they're preparing for the next Ironman competition. Planet Fitness tailored its entire business model to this 90%. Memberships start as low as $10 per month, making fitness accessible to people of all income levels. Their marketing campaigns emphasize body positivity and inclusivity, using relatable imagery of people of all shapes and sizes instead of chiseled fitness models. The gym's layout is designed to be user-friendly, with easy-to-use equipment and clear workout zones.

3. **Empowerment Through Small Wins and Continuous Growth** – While Planet Fitness is built on creating a comfortable, approachable environment,

they also emphasize the importance of growth—at each member's pace. Their trainers work with members to develop realistic goals, focusing on small, achievable wins that build confidence over time. This approach eliminates the pressure of extreme transformation stories and instead encourages steady, sustainable improvement. The company also invests in celebrating progress through creative programs and community recognition. In some locations, managers organize "Game Tape Playback" sessions during staff meetings, where they highlight funny or memorable moments of member success. Employees and members alike support each other's victories, fostering a strong sense of camaraderie. These small but meaningful acknowledgments create a ripple effect—members who start with modest goals often go on to achieve more because they feel empowered by their success and the support around them.

Planet Fitness's success story highlights the power of building a business around inclusivity, support, and sustainable progress. By focusing on a healthy culture, prioritizing the 90%, and empowering both members and staff through small wins, they have not only transformed individual lives but disrupted an entire industry. They created a gym where everyone feels they belong regardless of fitness level.

For business leaders, the lesson is clear: fostering an environment where all contributors feel valued can unlock hidden potential and drive long-term success. By focusing on culture, serving the majority, and promoting growth, you build a team (or membership base) that's stronger, more engaged, and ready to win—one small victory at a time. And just like those quiet, reliable field goals, those small wins add up to big results.

ENGAGING THE BENCH PLAYER

Here are five strategies to help leaders emphasize effort, re-silience, and sustainable performance:

1. **Conduct a Talent Audit.** Sit down with your team members and ask meaningful questions beyond their job descriptions. Discover hidden skills, passions, and past experiences that could align with your organizational goals.

2. **Design Stretch Assignments**. Give underutilized team members the chance to lead low-risk but high-visibility projects. These stretch assignments build confidence, encourage skill development, and prepare them for bigger roles.

3. **Implement Peer-Recognition Programs.** Create simple systems that allow colleagues to recognize each other's contributions. Over time, you'll see a pattern of impact players who operate behind the scenes but keep the team running strong.

4. **Celebrate Small Wins Publicly.** Develop rituals or communication channels where even minor achievements are celebrated, especially those from bench players. Consider things like "Silent Hero" awards or "Game Tape Playbacks" at team meetings.

5. **Create a Culture of Inclusion and Growth.** Make it clear through words and actions that everyone's

role matters. Eliminate fear-based management,
encourage curiosity, and provide consistent coaching so that when opportunity knocks, your bench is
ready to play.

By applying these strategies, leaders can ensure that their
team doesn't just rely on a few superstars but builds a
strong, deep roster ready for anything. That's the 90% advantage in action.

CORE PRINCIPLE II

Building Strategic Relationships Beyond the Scoreboard

*"I don't count sit-ups. I only
start counting when it starts hurting,
because they're the only ones that count."*

— Muhammad Ali

4.

Acceptance in Action: Creating a Positive Culture

What would it be worth to have a workplace where employees genuinely enjoy showing up? Where laughter isn't just allowed, it's encouraged. Where enthusiasm isn't a rare occurrence but an everyday reality. A place where energy is contagious, the atmosphere is inspiring, and productivity isn't just high—it's off the charts. As quantum physics suggests, energy attracts like energy. Negativity breeds more negativity, while positivity fuels even greater positivity. The culture you cultivate will determine what you attract.

How much easier would your job be if your team was motivated without constant prodding, if turnover was the exception instead of the rule, and if customer satisfaction soared because employees weren't just doing their jobs, they were excelling at them? Would it be worth fewer headaches, a more engaged workforce, and higher profits?

The answer? It would be priceless.

And yet, far too many workplaces take the opposite approach. No one enjoys being yelled at when they make a mistake. I've yet to meet someone who wakes up and thinks, "You know what would make my day? If I was called out in front of my peers for messing up." No one strives to fail in the office, on the field, or even in the arts. I've coached athletes at every level, from weekend warriors in youth sports to college and professional ranks. And

I have never once heard an athlete say, "Man, I really hope we lose today." Likewise, in theater, actors don't take the stage hoping to forget their lines; in marching band, musicians don't hope to step out of formation and trip over a tuba. People don't show up planning to fail. They show up wanting to win.

And yet, one of the most common management tactics in the workplace is fear-based motivation. In sports, it's the threat of the bench. At work, it's the looming fear of getting fired, demoted, or publicly shamed in a meeting. Too many leaders rely on punishment to "keep people in line," using micromanagement and criticism as their go-to playbook. The problem? Fear may produce short-term compliance, but it never inspires long-term excellence. A team that's afraid to fail will never take the risks needed to succeed.

> *"Fear may produce short-term compliance, but it never inspires long-term excellence."*

So, what's the alternative? It starts with culture. The kind that turns a workplace from a place of stress into a place of success. A culture where employees aren't looking over their shoulders in fear but looking ahead toward opportunities to grow, contribute, and win. And that? That's worth everything.

Now, imagine walking into an office where laughter mingles with the clatter of keyboards, where employees greet each other with genuine smiles, and where the energy is so palpable it could power the coffee machine. This isn't a scene from a feel-good movie; it's the daily reality at companies that have mastered the art of cultivating a positive workplace culture. But why should we, as managers and leaders, care about the mood lighting in the break room or the occasional office karaoke night? Because, as it turns out, fostering a positive culture isn't just about creating a pleasant atmosphere. It's a strategic move that can propel our teams to new heights of productivity and success.

A recent film encapsulating this concept is The Intern (2015), starring Robert De Niro and Anne Hathaway. In this heartwarming story, a 70-year-old widower, Ben Whittaker, joins an online fashion retailer as a senior intern. While his wisdom, experience, and positive attitude immediately begin to shift the workplace culture, not everyone welcomes him with open arms. Some employees feel threatened by his presence. They are skeptical of his old-school ways, dismissive of his insights, and even resistant to his calm and collected demeanor in a fast-paced, startup environment. To them, Ben represents a challenge to the status quo, a reminder that leadership isn't just about authority but about influence, relationships, and resilience.

Yet, despite the initial resistance, Ben's unwavering positivity and quiet leadership gradually break down the walls of skepticism. His ability to listen, support, and encourage those around him without pushing an agenda or demanding recognition creates a ripple effect. Initially overwhelmed and isolated, the CEO begins to lean on him for guidance. Colleagues who once dismissed him start seeking his advice. His presence fosters open communication, mutual respect, and a collaborative environment, increasing employee satisfaction and productivity. Ultimately, the culture shifts. Not through force but through the undeniable power of consistency, kindness, and authenticity.

This narrative is a testament to how a strong, positive culture doesn't just improve workplace dynamics. It transforms them. Even in environments where change is met with skepticism or resistance, genuine positivity can win people over when practiced consistently. That's the magic of culture. It may not happen immediately, but it becomes an unstoppable force when built intentionally. And if we could create that kind of workplace in our own organizations, what would it be worth?

The Business Case for Positivity: Why Culture Is More Than a Feel-Good Initiative

Let's return to the scoreboard mentality and its impact on culture. You know the drill. It's only about numbers, quotas, sales figures, and performance metrics that dominate every conversation. If it can't be measured, it must not matter. If it's not on the scoreboard, it doesn't count. Second place? Just the first loser. In corporate America, this mindset seems logical. After all, businesses need results, and tracking progress is essential. But when the scoreboard becomes the only focus, culture takes a backseat. There's nothing wrong with wanting to win, but when winning comes at all costs, it often leaves a trail of burnout, disengagement, and dysfunction in its wake.

As the winning-at-all-costs culture grows, it entangles the staff and ultimately takes priority over sustainability, morale, and teamwork. Employees stop thinking about the bigger picture. They begin making choices based on their own bottom line. They make decisions based solely on what will boost their short-term numbers. Need to hit that sales goal? Only if it benefits me. Need to cut costs? Slash resources and overwork employees. It's a cycle that might look great on paper until it doesn't.

When numbers become the sole measure of success, employees quickly shift from engaged contributors to overworked, stressed-out cogs in a relentless machine. The pressure to hit targets, meet quotas, and outperform last quarter's results overshadows creativity, innovation, and, most importantly, teamwork. Instead of fostering a culture of collaboration, the scoreboard mentality breeds cutthroat competition. "The unhealthy" kind where colleagues focus more on outpacing each other than actually working together.

It's like a basketball team where players are obsessed with padding their individual stats. They take impossible shots, hog the ball, and ignore open teammates. Someone might put up an impressive triple-double, but the team? They lose. Worse yet, morale tanks, resentment builds, and instead of a winning culture, you're left with a group of individuals fighting for personal victories at the expense of the collective goal. And when things go south, no one steps up to take ownership. Instead, it's the blame game. Finger-pointing at coworkers, badmouthing management, and avoiding responsibility like it's a contagious disease.

In a culture like this, where survival depends on out-shining the competition, what happens to the 90% of employees who already feel overlooked? The ones who aren't the top performers, the flashy rainmakers, or the "high potentials" being groomed for leadership? They see the game being rigged. They know they can't compete on the same level as the elite 10%. So what do they do? They check out. They disengage, keep their heads down, and do just enough to stay under the radar. Why push harder when the system only rewards the few at the top? Why invest more effort when credit is rarely given and the scoreboard never reflects their contributions? Instead of feeling like valued team members, they feel like placeholders. They are expendable, unappreciated, and ultimately disconnected from the company's success. And the moment a better opportunity comes along? They're gone. Not because they were bad employees but because the culture made it clear they were never really part of the team in the first place.

This kind of environment isn't just bad for employees; it's bad for your overall business. Burnt-out, disengaged employees don't bring their best ideas, they don't go the extra mile, and they certainly don't stick around for the long haul. A toxic, hyper-competitive workplace may get short-term wins, but in the end, it is unsustainable, unproductive, and, ultimately, a losing strategy.

Now, let's discuss the business case for positivity. Investing in a positive culture isn't just a feel-good initiative. It's a strategic advantage. The truth is, this kind of workplace isn't a fantasy. It's a choice. Companies that cultivate a positive culture reap rewards for performance, retention, and bottom-line success.

Before you roll your eyes and think this is all about singing "Kumbaya" and handing out participation trophies, let's be clear: this is not about creating a culture of mediocrity. The "everyone gets a ribbon" mentality that crept into youth sports in the millennial era doesn't translate well in business. In fact, it wreaks havoc in the corporate world when performance expectations aren't clear, accountability is lacking, and effort is rewarded regardless of outcomes. A strong positive culture is not about shielding people from challenges. On the contrary, it's about giving them the tools, motivation, and support to meet them head-on.

And guess what? Research proves that a strong, positive workplace culture isn't just good for morale. It delivers measurable business results. A study in the Journal of Applied Psychology[5] found that employees in supportive work environments perform better and stay longer. A 2022 Harvard Business Review study[6] confirmed that companies that prioritize a healthy culture see stronger financial results. Why? Because when employees feel valued and supported, they don't just punch in and punch out. They invest in the organization's success. They work harder, collaborate more, innovate fearlessly, and become ambassadors for your brand both inside and outside the company.

If you need further proof that a strong culture is a winning business strategy, just take a look at the cost of employee turnover. According to a 2023 Gallup poll,[7] disengaged employees cost U.S. businesses $1.9 trillion annually in lost productivity, rehiring, and training. And what drives disengagement? Toxic work environments, lack of recognition, and an absence of meaningful connections. When culture takes a backseat to numbers and metrics, employees start seeing work as a transaction rather than a mission. And when that happens, they leave at the first opportunity.

---

5   https://pmc.ncbi.nlm.nih.gov/articles/PMC9136218
6   professional.dce.harvard.edu/blog/how-to-build-and-improve-company-culture/
7   https://www.gallup.com/workplace/608675/new-workplace-employee-engagement-stagnates.aspx

The bottom line? Culture eats strategy for breakfast. Focusing solely on the scoreboard may get you some quick wins, but in the long run, it creates a toxic environment that burns out your best players. On the other hand, a positive culture builds a resilient, motivated, and high-performing team. One that's not just playing the game but playing to win together.

The best companies understand that positivity isn't a luxury. It's a competitive advantage. A positive workplace doesn't mean a lack of accountability. It means creating an environment where employees are motivated to succeed rather than afraid to fail. The difference between thriving and struggling companies often comes down to leadership's ability to cultivate a culture that drives performance without crushing people in the process.

The Ripple Effect

Robert Fulghum's book, All I Really Need to Know I Learned in Kindergarten, reminds us that life's most valuable lessons are not found in boardrooms or complex strategies. They are the simple principles we were taught as children. Share. Play fair. Say you're sorry when you hurt someone. Clean up your own mess. These basic ideas shape our lives and the world around us. Fulghum's wisdom speaks to the power of small actions and how they create ripples in our communities, relationships, and workplaces. Much like tossing a stone into a pond, every choice we make—kindness, integrity, or accountability—sends waves that influence those around us in ways we may never see. And that's where the real magic happens. Imagine the story below.

It was a quiet afternoon when Daniel wandered down to the small pond behind his grandfather's house. The air was still, the water perfectly smooth, like glass. He picked up a small stone, weighed it in his hand, and tossed it into the pond's center without much thought.

Plop.

Ripples spread outward in perfect circles, growing larger and larger, reaching the farthest edges of the water. The disturbance from that single stone set everything in motion. The sky's reflection shifted, a few startled fish darted away, and even the dragonfly resting on the surface lifted off in response.

"Funny thing, isn't it?" Daniel turned to see his grandfather watching him from the worn wooden bench nearby.

"What is?" Daniel asked, skipping another stone.

"The way one small action changes everything," his grandfather said, smiling. "You threw a single stone, but did you notice how far the ripples traveled? It didn't just affect the spot where it landed. It reached everything in its path."

Daniel watched the ripples until they faded, then returned to his grandfather. "So?"

"So," his grandfather said, leaning forward, "that's life. Every word you speak, and action you take sends ripples through the people around you. A kind word can spread just like those ripples, lifting someone's spirits and making their day a little brighter. A careless insult? That spreads too, just in a different way."

Daniel picked up another stone, this time holding it a little longer before tossing it into the water. The ripples spread again.

"You mean," he said slowly, "even small things I do can make a big difference?"

His grandfather chuckled. "Exactly. You may not always see where the ripples end, but they keep moving, touching people you may never even know." He patted Daniel's shoulder. "So the real question is—what kind of ripples do you want to create?"

Daniel didn't answer right away. He just watched the water, the last ripples of his second stone still moving across the surface. He picked up one more stone—not to toss just yet, but to remind himself that every action, no matter how small, had the power to shape the world around him.

So, what's the secret to creating a positive culture? It starts with you—and the ripple effect you have on others. Every action, every word, every decision is like a stone tossed into a pond, sending waves in every direction. Are you throwing pebbles of encouragement or boulders of stress and micromanagement? Are your ripples lifting people up or making them wish they had a life raft? The good news? You can always choose to change no matter what stones you've already thrown.

Because at the heart of every workplace culture is leadership. A company's culture is simply a reflection of the mindset of its leaders. That's why our first core principle, "Cultivating a Leadership Mindset," is so crucial. How you think about your people, purpose, and leadership doesn't just influence your success. It shapes the environment everyone else works in. If you see employees as problems to be managed, guess what? The culture will reflect that. Rigid, stressful, and filled with disengagement. But if you see them as "the key to success," you'll build a workplace where they feel valued, motivated, and empowered to do their best work.

In the end, the question isn't whether you're making waves. It's what kind of waves you're making. So, if you want a workplace that runs on trust, collaboration, and positivity, start by looking at the ripples you're sending out because culture isn't built in a day. But it is built every day!

> *"In the end, the question isn't whether you're making waves. It's what kind of waves you're making."*

If the world around us is a mirror, then the question becomes: What are we seeing, and what does it say about us? If we constantly encounter frustration, negativity, and disengagement in our workplace or personal life, it might be time to look inward. Are we projecting stress, doubt, or a lack of trust? Are we leading with fear instead of inspiration? The "Law of Reflection" reminds us that the external chaos we experience often stems from the mindset we bring into the situation. It's like walking around with a smudge on your glasses. If everything looks blurry, maybe the problem isn't the world but the lens you're looking through. The good news? We can clean the lens. By shifting our thoughts, approaches, and leadership styles, we don't just change ourselves. We change the energy we send out, the culture we create, and the ripples we set into motion.

As Gandhi famously said, "Be the change you want to see in the world." Shift your perspective, adjust your approach, and transform your thoughts. When you change yourself, you naturally influence and inspire those around you. And in doing so, you don't just change your world. You change the world.

Positivity as a Competitive Advantage: Keeping Your Talent in the Game

So, how do leaders create this kind of culture? It doesn't require a massive restructuring or an expensive corporate initiative. In fact, it's often the small, intentional actions that make the biggest difference. The daily choices that tell employees they are valued, heard, and supported. Encouraging open communication fosters an environment where team members feel safe to share ideas and concerns without fear of retribution. Recognizing and celebrating both big and small achievements builds morale and motivation. Promoting work-life balance through flexible work arrangements, mental health days, or initiatives like "Summer Mondays" helps employees recharge while maintaining productivity. Investing in professional development shows employees that their growth matters, increasing loyalty and engagement.

Success isn't just about hitting targets. It's about the people behind the numbers. Without a strong culture, relationships remain surface-level, and work feels transactional. But when culture is built on trust, appreciation, and shared purpose, people become more than just coworkers. They become a team.

Culture is the foundation upon which every great team is built. It sets the tone for how employees interact, how they approach challenges, and how they perform. It's the invisible force that determines whether people show up feeling inspired or simply obligated. More importantly, culture is not just an HR initiative. It is leadership in action.

How leaders think, communicate, and make decisions directly shapes the workplace environment. If you see your people as problems to be managed, the culture will reflect that. But if you recognize them as the 90% advantage, the everyday employees who show up, put in the work, and want to contribute you are already laying the foundation for something far more powerful: a thriving, positive workplace.

The power of embracing these core staff members cannot be overstated. Companies that focus only on high performers or star employees neglect the vast majority of their workforce. Yet, the real advantage isn't in an elite few. It is in the collective strength of the many. The unsung heroes. The ones who keep operations running, who show up every day, who do the work that often goes unnoticed. They are the backbone of any successful organization.

When leaders invest in coaching, developing, and appreciating all employees, they unlock hidden potential, increase engagement, and create a culture of ownership and accountability for everyone. They convey that success isn't just about chasing the next high performer. It's about building a workplace where everyone feels valued, empowered, and motivated to contribute.

Developing a positive workplace culture doesn't happen by accident. It's built intentionally through everyday leadership and the understanding that success isn't just about results. It's about the people behind them. A thriving culture doesn't come from policy handbooks or mission statements. It comes from the way leaders show up, the trust they build, and the example they set.

When you embrace the 90% advantage, you don't just transform the workplace. You elevate everyone in it.

Building a Culture Worth Showing Up For

Creating a positive workplace culture requires intention. It's not like free coffee and casual Fridays magically turn disengaged employees into top performers. It takes deliberate effort, consistent leadership, and a genuine investment in people. The secret sauce? A workplace built on core values, belonging & emotional safety, and positive communication. When these elements are woven into the very fabric of an organization, not just tacked onto a mission statement, employees don't just show up. They step up. They feel valued, motivated, and empowered to bring their best every day.

At the heart of any great culture are core values. The guiding tenets that define what a company stands for, how decisions are made, and, frankly, whether people actually enjoy working there or just tolerate it for the paycheck. Without clear values, companies operate like a GPS with no destination. Going somewhere, but no one really knows where. Core values that are actually lived out (and not just a laminated plaque in the breakroom) provide clarity, consistency, and connection. Employees don't just feel like they're clocking in. They feel like they are part of something bigger. When people believe in the mission, teamwork strengthens, trust deepens, and decision-making becomes less of a guessing game and more of a shared vision.

Culture isn't just a set of values written in a handbook.

It's the unspoken rhythm of an organization, the habits and behaviors that shape everyday interactions. That's why you can feel the energy when you walk into a great workplace. It's also why dysfunctional workplaces feel like walking into a meeting you weren't invited to. One of the simplest ways to define culture is through the saying, "This is the way we do things here." It's the invisible playbook that guides how people communicate, collaborate, and solve problems. When a company has a strong, positive culture, every new or seasoned employee understands the expectations in their job descriptions and how things get done. They know that respect is a given, feedback is constructive, and teamwork is the standard. not an afterthought. Setting this expectation early, especially with new hires, ensures that the culture isn't left to chance. It's intentional, reinforced, and lived out every day. When done right, it eliminates confusion, builds unity, and creates a workplace where people don't just survive. They thrive.

But let's be real. Core values alone won't cut it if employees feel like they don't belong. People don't just want to be on the team. They want to feel like they belong to it. Belonging and emotional safety create an environment where employees feel respected, heard, and safe enough to contribute without fear of being ridiculed, ignored, or thrown under the proverbial bus. When people worry about being judged or punished for speaking up, they shut down, innovation dries up, and engagement plummets. It's like a game of dodgeball. No one wants to get hit, so they stay on the sidelines. The best teams aren't necessarily the smartest. They are the ones who feel safe enough to share ideas, take risks, and admit when they need help.

> *"A positive culture isn't just a feel-good initiative. It is a competitive advantage."*

Finally, the glue that holds it all together is positive communication. The way people talk to each other in a company shapes its culture far more than any policy ever could. A workplace with clear, constructive, and respectful communication fosters trust, connection, and collaboration. On the flip side, toxic communication, gossip, passive-aggressive emails, and the dreaded "per my last email" nonsense creates resentment, disengagement, and high turnover. When leaders communicate openly, honestly, and with encouragement, employees feel heard, respected, and motivated. People work better when they're not secretly fuming over a snarky comment in a team meeting.

A positive culture isn't just a feel-good initiative. It is a competitive advantage. Companies that prioritize core values, belonging & emotional safety, and positive communication don't just have happier employees. They have more productive, engaged, and loyal teams. Culture isn't built suddenly, and it's certainly not something you can fake. It's something that is modeled, reinforced, and cultivated every single day.

Because, at the end of the day, culture isn't just what you say. It's what you do. And if you do it right? Your employees will show up with purpose, passion, and the drive to make your company better.

SAS INSTITUTE – THE POWER OF POSITIVE CULTURE FROM THE START

SAS Institute, a global leader in analytics software, stands as a shining example of a company that understood the value of a positive culture from the start. Unlike many organizations that have had to course-correct after facing toxic work environments, SAS has consistently prioritized employee well-being, engagement, and long-term satisfaction. This commitment has paid off—resulting in remarkably low turnover, industry-leading innovation, and sustained profitability.

From its founding in 1976, SAS co-founder and long-time CEO Dr. Jim Goodnight recognized that investing in people was just as important as investing in technology. His philosophy was simple: happy, supported employees create better products, deliver better service, and ultimately drive business success. This approach has made SAS one of the most admired workplaces in the world—a company that attracts and retains top talent while maintaining an unwavering focus on innovation and excellence.

SAS's positive workplace culture isn't about gimmicks or surface-level perks but a deeply embedded philosophy that values people first. Here's how the company has structured its culture to ensure long-term success:

1. **Employee-Centric Benefits:** SAS was one of the first companies to offer on-site healthcare, childcare,

and fitness centers, reinforcing its commitment to work-life balance. By reducing external stressors, employees could focus more on creativity and productivity.

2. **Trust and Autonomy**: Unlike many corporate environments that operate with rigid policies and micromanagement, SAS fosters a culture of trust and flexibility. Employees have the freedom to approach their work in ways that make sense to them, leading to higher engagement and innovation.

3. **Professional Development**: SAS continuously invests in employee growth, providing opportunities for learning, mentorship, and skill-building. The result? A workforce that is highly skilled and deeply loyal to the company.

4. **No Layoff Policy**: One of the most remarkable aspects of SAS's culture is its commitment to job security. While many tech companies have gone through cycles of mass layoffs, SAS has maintained a "no layoff" policy, ensuring employees feel secure and valued—further boosting loyalty and retention.

The impact of SAS's commitment to positive workplace culture is undeniable:

1. Turnover rates at SAS remain at just 4%–5%, significantly lower than the 20%+ industry average in tech. This means fewer hiring costs, stronger institutional knowledge, and a highly experienced workforce. Consistently ranked as one of the "Best

Places to Work" by Fortune and Forbes.

2. Innovation at the Forefront: SAS's emphasis on employee well-being translates directly into higher creativity and productivity. Employees are not bogged down by burnout or workplace stress, allowing them to focus on AI, data analytics, and machine learning breakthroughs.

3. Financial Success: Unlike many tech firms that rely on rapid expansion and volatile growth strategies, SAS has maintained steady, profitable growth for decades, reinforcing the idea that a long-term focus on culture drives sustainable success.

SAS proves that positive culture isn't just an HR buzzword—it's a business strategy that pays off. Here's what other companies can learn from SAS's success:

1. ***Invest in Employee Well-Being*** – Employees who feel supported perform better. Providing benefits that reduce life stress (like healthcare, childcare, and mental health support) leads to greater engagement and productivity.

2. ***Foster a Culture of Trust*** – Micromanagement crushes creativity and motivation. Giving employees autonomy and flexibility allows them to take ownership of their work and deliver better results.

3. ***Commit to Stability*** – Companies that show employees they are valued beyond short-term profits create long-term loyalty, reducing turnover costs and boosting performance.

4. ***Make Culture a Business Strategy*** – Positive workplace culture isn't just about making employees happy—it directly impacts innovation, retention, and financial success.

While many companies have had to reinvent themselves after struggling with toxic work environments, SAS got it right from the start. By prioritizing employee well-being, trust, and stability, SAS has built one of the best workplaces in the world and established itself as a leader in analytics software for nearly 50 years.

SAS proves that a strong culture is more than a feel-good initiative—a business advantage leading to long-term success. And in today's fast-changing world, companies that fail to invest in culture will struggle to compete against those that get it right from the start—just like SAS.

BUILDING A POSITIVE CULTURE

Here are five strategies to help you build a workplace culture that attracts great people, energizes teams, and sustains high performance:

1. *Lead with Optimism, not Fear*. Your energy sets the tone for your entire team. Show up with purpose, encouragement, and belief in your people. Recognize that fear-based leadership might produce compliance, but positivity produces commitment. Encourage progress, celebrate small wins, and replace micromanagement with empowerment.

2. *Make Culture Everyone's Responsibility*. Culture doesn't live in HR manuals or mission statements. It lives in daily actions and decisions. Encourage all team members to model core values, call out toxic behavior, and support one another in living out the organization's mission. Reinforce culture at every level—from onboarding to performance reviews.

3. *Promote Psychological Safety*. Create an environment where people feel safe to speak up, admit mistakes, and share ideas without fear of judgment. Prioritize emotional safety just as much as physical safety. This means leading with empathy, listening with curiosity, and responding without blame.

4. *Communicate with Clarity and Consistency*. Positive cultures are built on trust, and trust is built

through clear, consistent, and constructive communication. Ditch passive-aggressive emails and vague feedback. Say what you mean, mean what you say, and deliver it with respect.

5. ***Design Culture Moments That Stick***. Rituals reinforce culture. Whether it's shout-outs in team meetings, creative recognitions like the "Silent Hero Award," or shared moments like "Game Tape Playback," design rituals that celebrate your values and make positivity visible. These moments create belonging and elevate everyday contributions into cultural touchstones.

A positive culture isn't accidental. It's intentional, strategic, and worth every ounce of effort. When leaders invest in people, they don't just boost morale. They build a winning team that thrives together.

*"It's never a mistake to care for someone.
That's always a good thing!"*

— Linda in Radio

5.

Leading With Empathy

Learning opportunities have a funny way of showing up. Sometimes, they crash down on us like a rogue wave—loud, messy, and impossible to ignore. Other times, they tiptoe softly, waiting for the right moment when we're paying attention. Leadership is one of those lessons that often sneaks up on us, even when the world practically screams about its importance.

There are thousands of books on leadership—some legendary, like The 21 Irrefutable Laws of Leadership by John C. Maxwell, Good to Great by Jim Collins, and The Five Dysfunctions of a Team by Patrick Lencioni. There are experts, opinions, and enough TED Talks to last a lifetime. Colleges, companies, and institutions are always on the lookout for leaders. And yet, one of the toughest questions I ask high school and college athletes is this: "By a show of hands, how many of you are a leader?"

Cue the awkward silence. They glance at each other, waiting for anyone to go first. Eventually, one or two hesitant hands creep up. The rest? They sit there, unsure. It's mind-boggling. Why don't they see themselves as leaders?

So, I push a little. "Why didn't you raise your hand?"

The most common answer? They're worried about how they'll be perceived. They don't want to come across as arrogant, cocky, or full of themselves. And honestly, that makes sense. Nobody wants to be "that person" who declares themselves a leader only to be side-eyed by their peers.

Amazingly, this isn't just a high school problem. Ask a room full of adults, and you'll get the same hesitant silence. Why?

The Leadership Identity Crisis

Part of the issue stems from the outdated belief that "leaders are born, not made." This perspective suggests that you're disqualified for life if you weren't labeled as a leader early on. Additionally, societal stereotypes often associate leadership with traditionally masculine traits, leading many to feel they don't fit the mold. Leadership is frequently equated with assertiveness, dominance, and decisiveness. Qualities that, historically, have been attributed more to men than women. Because of this, many individuals hesitate to claim leadership, even when they demonstrate the necessary skills.

Research shows that men and women perceive leadership—and themselves as leaders—differently. Studies indicate that men are more likely to overestimate their leadership abilities, while women tend to underestimate theirs, a phenomenon commonly referred to as the confidence gap.[8] Women are also less likely to self-identify as leaders due to implicit biases that equate leadership with male-dominated qualities. These biases create a vicious cycle. Women hesitate to step into leadership roles, reinforcing the stereotype that leadership is a male trait, making it even harder for future generations of women to see themselves as leaders.[9]

And let's not forget about cultural conditioning. From a young age, boys are often encouraged to take charge, be

---

8   https://www.aauw.org/resources/research/barrier-bias
9   https://sajip.co.za/index.php/sajip/article/view/1704

bold, and speak up, while girls are praised for being cooperative, kind, and humble. Fast forward 20 years, and it's no wonder that many men feel comfortable stepping into leadership roles while many women hesitate even when they're equally or more qualified.

This early conditioning doesn't just influence attitudes; it builds the scaffolding for who gets to climb the ladder in the first place. Think of leadership as a race where some runners start closer to the finish line, not because they're faster, but because the course was paved differently for them from the very beginning. According to a 2023 report by Catalyst,[10] women held only 10.4% of CEO positions in Fortune 500 companies. Less than 11% of the top seats at the biggest companies in the country are held by women. Meanwhile, men continue to dominate the C-suite, not necessarily because they are more capable, but because they've been groomed from a young age to see leadership as their lane. Boys are often encouraged to take the lead; girls are taught to support. So, while both genders enter the workforce with ambition, confidence tends to favor those who've been conditioned to believe they belong in front.

The reluctance to claim leadership isn't just a gender issue. It's a broader societal one that affects people across all walks of life. Many individuals, regardless of gender, background, or experience, shy away from leadership roles not because they lack the capability but because they fear the perception that comes with stepping forward. For some, the idea of identifying as a leader feels synonymous with being seen as arrogant, bossy, or self-important. Others

---

10   Catalyst. (2023). Women CEOs of the S&P 500. https://www.catalyst.org/research/women-ceos-of-the-sp-500/

worry they'll be viewed as overreaching, especially if they don't hold a certain title, degree, or years of experience. There's an underlying anxiety about how colleagues, peers, or even friends will respond. Will they think I'm trying too hard? Will they assume I think I'm better than everyone else?

This internal tug-of-war keeps many people from stepping into roles where they could have a significant impact. Instead, they play it safe, waiting for permission, a formal invitation, or a title that finally makes it acceptable to lead. But here's the irony: leadership is often most powerful when it's not about power at all. It's not about being the loudest in the room or having all the answers. It's about influence, initiative, and the ability to help others thrive.

Yet, despite this truth, many people keep their hands down, their ideas quiet, and their potential tucked away in fear of judgment. And it raises a critical question. If leadership is so essential to thriving teams, organizations, and communities, why have we made it feel so exclusive? Why have we turned it into something people hesitate to claim rather than something they're proud to grow into?

The problem isn't a shortage of capable leaders. It's a shortage of people who believe they're allowed to lead. And that's exactly the shift we need to make if we want to activate the 90% advantage—creating a culture where everyday people are encouraged, empowered, and equipped to lead in their own authentic way.

Where's the Leadership Training?

Let's rewind to high school. At some point, you probably figured out that colleges love leadership. But how much actual leadership education did you receive? You spent years studying history, writing essays, solving for x, and dissecting frogs. You probably even memorized verb conjugations in a foreign language you barely remember. Yet, in all that time, how many courses specifically focused on leadership? How many years of leadership training did you receive?

If you were lucky, maybe you had a single unit in an elective class. If you were a team captain or club officer, you might have picked up leadership skills through experience, but formal training? Probably not.

Fast forward to college. Maybe you had a semester-long course or picked up leadership skills through extracurriculars. But chances are, it was all hands-on, trial by fire. You figured it out as you went. What worked, what didn't, and what made people roll their eyes behind your back?

At this stage, you were likely more aware that leadership mattered. You were more proactive. More inclined to step up. You allowed yourself to be seen as a leader. But were you getting the kind of leadership training that actually prepared you for the real world?

Because let's be honest—reading a book about leadership and actually being a leader are two different things. Discussions are great, but where's the real foundation? What are the core skills you need? And most importantly, why is it still so hard to confidently raise your hand?

> *"Leadership is a skill. One that anyone willing to step up, take responsibility, and improve those around them can develop, practice, and master."*

Redefining Leadership - Turning Good People into Great Performers

If leadership is truly for everyone, regardless of gender, background, or personality, it's time to redefine what leadership looks like. Leadership isn't reserved for the loudest voice in the room, the title on a business card, or the person who naturally commands attention. It's not just for the charismatic CEO, the outspoken team captain, or the born extrovert. Leadership is a skill. One that anyone willing to step up, take responsibility, and improve those around them can develop, practice, and master.

There once was a time in a person's career when "paying your dues" wasn't just expected. It was the "unwritten law of the workplace." Fresh ideas were not welcomed until you had enough years under your belt, and speaking up too soon could get you labeled as naïve, arrogant, or "not ready." Some directors and CEOs would even say it outright: "I don't want to hear from you until you've been working here for at least three years. Nothing you say to me is relevant. You need experience, and that takes time."

This mindset didn't just stifle innovation. It shut people down before they even had a chance to contribute. It conveyed that talent only comes with tenure, that fresh perspectives are meaningless, and that leadership is reserved for those who have simply waited their turn. But times have changed. The best organizations no longer rely on hierarchical gatekeeping to determine whose voice matters. Instead, they recognize that ideas don't have a tenure requirement and leadership potential doesn't magically appear after a set number of years. The future of work belongs to those who value experience and fresh thinking in equal measure because the best ideas can come from anywhere, regardless of how long someone has been on the job.

And that's where the 90% advantage comes in.

Most leadership development focuses on the top 10%. The all-stars, the MVPs, the natural-born leaders who seem destined for greatness. Maybe you have been identified as one of those high potential top 10% elite members within the company. Good for you. That really is an accomplishment. But real teams don't just win on the backs of a few elite players. They win because every player contributes. Championships aren't won on talent alone. They're won through effort, discipline, and the ability to make those around you better.

This is where many organizations get it wrong. They're focused on the scoreboard, the results, the top performers, the next big star. While overlooking the everyday plays that make victory possible. They celebrate the game-winning shot but ignore the relentless effort that kept the team in the game. They reward the flashiest player but forget that leadership is just as much about the role players who set the screen, make the extra pass, and put in the work that doesn't make the highlight reel.

The biggest opportunity for growth in any organization isn't in turning great people into superstars. It's in turning good people into great performers. Leadership isn't about managing the elite few. It's about unlocking the potential in the many. The teams that succeed in business and sports are the ones that elevate everyone, not just the chosen few.

This is the foundation of the 90% advantage. The idea is that real success in leadership isn't about identifying a handful of exceptional people but about raising the bar for everyone. It's about recognizing that leadership isn't just about the final score. It's about the daily commitment to effort, execution, and making your teammates better. Years of experience are irrelevant.

In sports, effort is the great equalizer. You may not be the fastest or the strongest, but you can always control how hard you work. The same is true in leadership. Not everyone starts as a leader, but anyone can become one through effort, consistency, and a willingness to step up. The best leaders aren't necessarily the most talented. They're the ones who make their team better, no matter their role.

Believe it or not, there isn't just one type of leader. Some people think leaders must be either "elected" or "selected," as if leadership is some exclusive club with a VIP list. But some of the best leaders don't even realize they're leading. They're too busy making everyone around them better.

Leadership isn't about fitting into a rigid mold. It comes in all shapes, styles, and decibel levels. Some leaders are loud and commanding, rallying the troops with an energy that could wake the dead. Others are quiet and steady, letting their actions do the talking while everyone else scrambles to keep up. Some lead with raw emotion, wearing their passion on their sleeve, while others use humor to lighten the load and make the journey more bearable. Some leaders inspire through wisdom, those who connect through faith or spirituality, and those who simply roll up their sleeves and get the job done. Leading by example without ever needing a title.

Leadership is also not about a "one size fits all" deal. When organizations embrace different leadership styles, letting each person's unique strengths shine, that's when the real magic happens. And not just in small doses. We're talking large quantities. The Costco-sized magic of leadership. Because the more diverse the leadership styles, the stronger and more adaptable the team.

In 2007, as the Boston Celtics were rebuilding their roster, head coach Doc Rivers sought a unifying philosophy to bond his newly assembled team. During a lunch break at a Marquette University Board meeting, Rivers spoke with Stephanie Russell, the university's executive director for mission and identity. Russell introduced Rivers to the Ubuntu proverb, which translates to "I am because we are." This African philosophy emphasizes the interconnectedness of individuals and the belief that one's humanity is tied to the humanity of others.[11]

Inspired by this philosophy, Rivers didn't just introduce it to the Celtics. He made it the foundation of their culture. He laid out a simple but powerful truth in their first team meeting. Individual success is meaningless without the success of the group. It wasn't about one superstar carrying the team. It was about every player embracing their role, trusting one another, and committing to something bigger than themselves. Ubuntu wasn't just a slogan. It was a mindset that transformed good players into great teammates and great teammates into champions.

This philosophy embodies the 90% advantage. The idea that true success isn't about a select few outperforming the rest. It's about elevating everyone. The Celtics' championship wasn't won solely on talent. It was won through

---

11   https://www.celticslife.com/2010/07/i-am-because-we-are-flashback-on-ubuntu.html

trust, selflessness, and a belief that each player's contribution mattered, whether they were a starter or coming off the bench. When organizations and leaders embrace this mentality, they unlock potential in places they might otherwise overlook.

The Golden Rule of Leadership (It's Not What You Think)

If leadership isn't just for the naturally gifted, the extroverted, or the hand-picked few, then what does it take to bring out the best in the 90%? How do we shift the focus from exclusive leadership to inclusive leadership? Where every individual is given the chance to develop, grow, and contribute at a higher level?

The answer lies in understanding how to coach, support, and engage the everyday workforce. The people who may not see themselves as leaders yet but who, with the right guidance, can become the foundation of a thriving team and organization. The Golden Rule teaches us to "do unto others as you would want them to do to you," emphasizing empathy and fairness in our interactions. Applying this to leadership means creating opportunities for others as we would hope for opportunities ourselves. We must create an environment where individuals can develop, grow, and contribute just as we would want for ourselves.

Let's play out this rule in real time. Imagine a manager who wants to receive public recognition and then uses that approach with everyone on the team. Following this Golden Rule, the manager habitually praises employees in front of the entire company, thinking they are uplifting and motivating them. Just as he wants for himself. One day, after publicly acknowledging a team member's hard work during a company-wide meeting, he notices that instead of looking proud, one of the employees looks uncomfortable, even embarrassed. Later, the employee privately expresses that they prefer one-on-one recognition and feel overwhelmed by the spotlight. The manager's good intentions backfired. Not because recognition was unwelcome but because the method of delivering it didn't align with the employee's preferences.

> *"A truly effective leader takes the time to learn how each team member prefers to receive feedback, appreciation, and support."*

This is where the Platinum Rule comes in. "Do unto others as they want to be treated." True leadership evolves by understanding that not everyone wants to be treated like us. A truly effective leader takes the time to learn how each team member prefers to receive feedback, appreciation, and support. By doing so, they shift from well-intended but misguided leadership to personalized leadership, where every individual is empowered in a way that resonates with them.

This requires leaders to offer opportunities and understand what each individual truly needs to thrive. Coaching, supporting, and engaging the everyday workforce means recognizing their unique strengths, aspirations, and challenges. Not just treating them as we would want to be treated, but as they want to be treated. By shifting from exclusive leadership to inclusive leadership, we empower those who may not yet see themselves as leaders to realize their potential, becoming the foundation of a thriving team and organization.

The Power of Empathy: Developing a Healthy Culture

Many leaders mistake sympathy for empathy. Just as they mistake hearing for listening. Sympathy acknowledges someone's struggles but keeps a level of emotional distance. It says, "I feel bad for you." Empathy takes it a step further. It listens, understands, and responds with meaningful action. It says, "I see you. I understand you. I'm here with you." This distinction is critical in leadership. A sympathetic leader may notice an overwhelmed employee and offer a kind word, but without the ability to listen actively and engage thoughtfully, that support often stops at the surface. An empathetic leader leans in, asks insightful questions, and works collaboratively to find solutions that address the root cause.

Consider a leader managing a high-performing team where one member starts missing deadlines. A sympathetic response might be, "I know you're stressed. I'm sorry it's been tough." It's well-intended, but it doesn't go beyond acknowledgment. However, an empathetic leader with strong listening skills takes the time to ask, "What's going on? How can I support you?" Instead of making assumptions, they listen deeply to understand whether the issue stems from workload, lack of clarity, personal struggles, or burnout. By engaging with empathy and applying active listening, the leader doesn't just check the box of "showing concern." They create a real, lasting impact. This approach helps the individual and reinforces a workplace culture where employees feel seen, valued, and supported in a way that makes a difference.

In leadership, empathy is the foundation of a thriving workplace culture, one that fosters trust, engagement, and a shared commitment to success. Without it, leaders are just managers with fancier titles and more meetings on their calendars.

While the Platinum Rule teaches us to treat others as they want to be treated, true leadership requires something deeper: Understanding and responding to the needs of those we lead, even when they differ from our own. This is where empathy becomes a defining characteristic of great leadership. It is also where things get tricky. It's easy to assume that what works for us will work for everyone else. But people are not one-size-fits-all, and leadership isn't about handing out the same standard-issue pep talk like free T-shirts at a corporate retreat.

For instance, Mark is a well-meaning but oblivious manager. He thought he was building camaraderie by starting every Monday morning meeting with an icebreaker. His favorite? Asking everyone to share what they did over the weekend. Except that half the team dreaded it. The introverts prayed they'd disappear into their coffee mugs, the new hire fresh out of college had no idea how to make "watched six hours of Netflix" sound professional, and one employee, who had just gone through a rough breakup, wasn't exactly eager to discuss their weekend activities. While Mark thought he was creating an engaging culture, he created Monday Morning Anxiety.™ An actual term, also known as the "Monday blues." A common feeling of sadness, dread, or lethargy that occurs at the start of the workweek. It's a natural response to the transition from weekend relaxation to work demands.

His intention was good, but intention alone doesn't build a healthy culture. Impact does. His effort to foster engagement was a step in the right direction, but without awareness and adaptability, it backfired. Creating a culture where people feel included and valued requires more than just good ideas. It requires deeper leadership skills and training that equip managers to read the room, recognize different communication styles, and adjust accordingly.

Let's return to our days in the classroom. Many teachers begin their day with a morning meeting that allows students to share what's on their minds. It helps build connections, sets the tone for the day, and gives students a sense of belonging. Adults are no different. But while the intent behind these practices remains valuable, the execution must evolve to fit the realities of the workplace.

Unlike a classroom where participation is encouraged but not always required, employees have different comfort levels, personalities, and work styles that must be considered. A well-meaning attempt at fostering openness can quickly turn into forced vulnerability, leaving some employees disengaged rather than connected. The key isn't just implementing a routine. It's understanding how people want to engage and creating an environment where they choose to participate rather than feeling obligated.

Had he led with empathy, Mark would have realized that not everyone enjoys a group therapy session before 9 a.m. Instead of assuming what his team wanted, he could have asked, listened, and adapted—maybe allowing employees to contribute in different ways, like submitting anonymous weekend highlights or simply starting with a quick check-in that let people opt in or out.

This is the difference between leading with good intentions and leading with empathy. The best leaders don't just act on what they think is right. They take the time to understand what is right for the people they serve. Empathy isn't about assuming. It's about asking. It's not about projecting your preferences but respecting others' perspectives. And most importantly, it's about creating an environment where people feel valued, not just managed.

The Ripple Effect of an Empathetic Leader

An empathetic leader doesn't just impact individuals. They shape the entire organization. When people feel truly seen, heard, and supported, they naturally become more engaged, motivated, and committed. They don't just clock in and out. They bring their best selves to the work they do. As Oprah Winfrey puts it, "Leadership is about empathy. It is about relating to and connecting with people to inspire and empower their lives." That's the secret. Great leaders don't just manage tasks. They connect with people in a way that makes them want to go the extra mile. And, if you are able to knowingly strive to connect with the 90%, imagine the advantage you will have.

Empathy is not a soft skill. It is a powerful leadership tool that differentiates good managers from great leaders. It builds loyalty, enhances collaboration, and drives performance, not through fear or pressure (the scoreboard) but through genuine connection and understanding (mindset and kindness). A workplace built on empathy transforms leadership from a position of authority into a role of service. Where the goal isn't just to delegate but to uplift, empower, and inspire. It's not about being nice for the sake of it. It's about unlocking performance through connection. When people feel valued, they work harder. Not because they have to but because they want to.

This is why the best leaders aren't just focused on results. They focus on the people who create those results. It's about shifting from a "manage and control" mindset to a "coach and support" approach. Microsoft CEO Satya Nadella nails it when he says, "Empathy isn't just a 'nice to have.' It's at the center of innovation." The truth is, when leaders lead with empathy, they don't just build stronger teams. They turn good people into great performers. And that's the kind of leadership that creates lasting success.

Culture Creators:
Leading for All, Not Just the Few

Great leaders don't just manage people. They shape the culture that determines whether employees are thriving or just surviving. A culture creator is a leader who intentionally shapes the workplace environment to bring out the best in their people. They don't just enforce policies or chase performance metrics. They set the tone, model behaviors, and create a space where employees feel valued, empowered, and motivated to contribute. A culture creator understands that company culture isn't built on words in a handbook but in daily interactions, leadership actions, and how people feel when they appear to work. They prioritize trust, inclusion, and engagement, ensuring that every team member, not just the top performers, has the opportunity to grow and thrive. Instead of forcing people to conform to a rigid system, they build a culture that adapts to and amplifies the strengths of the people within it, creating an environment where both individuals and the organization can succeed together.

> *"Great leaders don't just manage people. They shape the culture that determines whether employees are thriving or just surviving."*

Google, known for being obsessed with data, wanted to figure out what truly makes a team thrive. So, in 2012, they launched Project Aristotle, a deep dive into team performance, analyzing over 180 teams to uncover the secret formula behind success. They assumed it would come down to things like IQ, skill sets, or having a few rockstar performers leading the charge. But what they actually found was something much deeper and far more human.[12]

At the heart of their findings was psychological safety. The idea was that the best teams were not necessarily the ones with the smartest people but ones where everyone felt safe enough to speak up, share ideas, and take risks without fear of judgment.[13] The most effective teams were not built on competition or hierarchy but on trust, respect, and open dialogue. This means the best leaders were not the ones barking orders from the top but the ones who cre-

---

12 https://rework.withgoogle.com/en/guides/understanding-team-effectiveness
13 https://psychsafety.com/googles-project-aristotle

ated an environment where everyone felt heard and valued. This is also a quality of a highly effective teacher. Someone who knows how to cultivate a space where people feel safe enough to explore, question, and grow. After all, good leaders are also great teachers. They don't just direct; they develop. They don't just instruct; they inspire.

Project Aristotle didn't just reveal that people need to feel safe to contribute. It showed that leaders and teammates need authentic listening. Everyone needs to take the time to listen for that culture to take root. When people feel like their ideas are heard, not just nodded at in a meeting while someone checks their phone, they become more engaged, more creative, and more invested in the team's success.[14] The study found that the best teams had leaders who weren't just making decisions from the top down but were actively listening, responding, and adapting to the needs of the group.

What does this mean for leaders today? It signifies that the old-school way of only listening to the most outspoken or senior voices is outdated and ineffective. It recognizes that ideas don't have a tenure requirement, and leadership potential doesn't magically appear after a set number of years. They build workplaces where experience is valued, but so is curiosity, fresh thinking, and the courage to speak up. No matter where you sit in the organizational chart, employees are hired because of what they bring to the table. So don't stifle their contributions by making them feel like they need permission to speak. If you want innovation, engagement, and real momentum, you need to make sure everyone's voice is heard.

---

14 https://www.leaderfactor.com/learn/project-aristotle-psychological-safety

Real leadership isn't about managing from above. It's about elevating the 90%. Too often, organizations only tap into a fraction of their workforce, relying on the usual faces to drive innovation. But the true competitive advantage lies in the 90%. The employees are not always the loudest but are full of ideas, insights, and untapped potential.[15] If leaders take the time to foster psychological safety and practice authentic listening, they unlock the full power of their teams.

The takeaway? If you want to lead with empathy and build a culture of success, start by making your team feel safe to contribute. Listen—not just to respond, but to understand. Create an environment where ideas flow freely, where taking risks is encouraged, and where leadership isn't reserved for the few but embraced by the many. The best teams aren't built on titles or tenure. They are built on trust, engagement, and the belief that every voice matters.

A culture creator builds a workplace that thrives on empathy-driven leadership, where people feel safe, valued, and motivated to contribute their best work. They foster psychological safety, ensuring employees can share ideas, ask questions, and even admit mistakes without feeling like they just walked onto an episode of Shark Tank. They champion inclusion, where diverse perspectives aren't just accepted but actively embraced, and leadership meets people where they are. Most importantly, they cultivate collaboration, where people work together because they want to, not because they're trying to decode a passive-aggressive email. A culture creator understands that a great workplace

---

15 https://iremdenver.starchapter.com/images/downloads/Documents/project_aristotle_comprehensive.pdf

isn't built by accident. It's shaped with intention, empathy, and a commitment to bringing out the best in everyone. And that's how good people become great performers and how great workplaces become unstoppable.

A CASE STUDY

THE PHOENIX SUNS – FROM TOXIC CULTURE TO CHAMPIONSHIP CONTENDER

In sports, just like in business, talent alone doesn't guarantee success. Culture plays a massive role in building a winning organization. The Phoenix Suns struggled to find consistency on the court for years despite having talented players. But the real issue wasn't in the locker room. It was at the top.

For nearly two decades, the Suns were led by owner Robert Sarver and CEO Jason Rowley, both of whom were at the center of a leadership culture that was increasingly toxic, controlling, and damaging to the organization's long-term success. Reports surfaced of hostile work environments, instances of racism, misogyny, and a culture of fear that stifled innovation, trust, and collaboration. Employees described a workplace where speaking up could cost them their jobs and where micromanagement and intimidation were the norm.

While the team had flashes of success, they could never build sustained excellence. A direct result of a dysfunctional culture. Much like an underperforming business, they had the right "employees" (players), but the leadership at the top created an environment where people couldn't do their best work.

The breaking point came in 2021 when ESPN published an investigative report detailing numerous allegations against Sarver and his leadership team. With over

70 current and former employees speaking out about the toxic workplace, the NBA was forced to step in. After an independent investigation, Sarver was suspended for a year and fined $10 million, and amid mounting pressure, he announced his decision to sell the team.

But the real transformation didn't start with just removing Sarver. It started when the organization realized that culture had to be intentionally rebuilt from the ground up. Enter Mat Ishbia, a billionaire mortgage executive who bought the team in early 2023 with a clear vision for leadership transformation. Ishbia understood that businesses and sports teams thrive not through micromanagement but through trust, empowerment, and psychological safety.

Under Ishbia's leadership, the Suns made an intentional shift away from the command-and-control leadership style that had plagued the organization. Instead, they embraced a leadership model aligned with Google's Project Aristotle—focusing on psychological safety, authentic listening, and empathy as core drivers of high performance.

This redefined what success looked like from the inside out. By prioritizing trust and psychological safety over hierarchy and control, the organization created space for people to bring their full selves to work. Employees no longer felt the need to operate in fear or silence. Instead, they were encouraged to contribute ideas, challenge assumptions, and take ownership of their work. When people feel heard and respected, they're not just more productive. They're more creative, more collaborative, and more committed. That's when an organization starts to perform at a level far beyond what top-down authority could ever achieve.

The impact of this cultural transformation was immediate. Internally, employee morale dramatically improved as trust in leadership was rebuilt. Departments that once felt stifled under micromanagement began to flourish, and collaboration across the organization became a key strength rather than a weakness.

On the court, the Suns continued to build a winning culture, attracting high-profile players and strengthening their reputation as a serious championship contender. The shift in leadership had a direct impact on their ability to build long-term success rather than just chasing short-term wins.

1. ***Creating Psychological Safety*** – One of the first major shifts was fostering an environment where employees felt safe to speak up, share ideas, and contribute without fear of retaliation. In the past, employees—whether in the front office or player development—often stayed silent rather than challenge decisions. Now, leadership encouraged open dialogue, welcomed feedback, and promoted a culture where even junior-level employees had a voice.

2. ***Moving Away from Micromanagement*** – Micromanagement had been one of the Suns' biggest issues, with past leadership controlling even minor details, second-guessing staff, and making unilateral decisions without collaboration. Under the new structure, leaders empowered employees and coaching staff to take ownership of their roles, make decisions, and contribute at a higher level.

3. ***Authentic Listening & Employee Empowerment***
   – The Suns' leadership team also recognized that
   employees needed to feel heard. Leadership began
   conducting regular town halls, feedback sessions,
   and one-on-one meetings to truly understand what
   was needed at all levels of the organization. This
   wasn't just about listening for the sake of it—it was
   about taking action based on employee insights.

The Phoenix Suns' transformation is a perfect case study for
any business struggling with a top-down, command-and-
control leadership style. The lesson is clear: No amount of
talent can overcome bad leadership. A toxic workplace stifles innovation, kills motivation, and keeps organizations in
mediocrity cycles. By embracing principles of psychological
safety, authentic listening, and empowering employees, the
Suns turned a dysfunctional organization into a thriving,
competitive force. Businesses that fail to recognize the importance of culture will eventually pay the price, whether
through lost talent, poor performance, or public scandals.

LEADING WITH EMPATHY

Here are five strategies to help you lead with empathy, develop authentic connections, and elevate the 90% of your workforce who are ready to thrive:

1. ***Shift from the Golden Rule to the Platinum Rule***. Don't treat people how you want to be treated. Treat them how they want to be treated. Learn what makes each person feel seen and supported. That shift in mindset changes how you communicate, coach, and connect across the board.

2. ***Practice Authentic Listening.*** Listening to respond is a habit. Listening to understand is a skill. Drop the multitasking, stop rehearsing your reply, and be fully present. People can tell when you're only half-listening—and they act accordingly.

3. ***Cultivate Psychological Safety***. Create a culture where employees feel safe to speak up, take risks, and even fail without fear of judgment. Make space for vulnerability and be the first to model it. When leaders admit mistakes, it gives everyone else permission to be honest and human.

4. ***Embrace Feedback as a Gift.*** Encourage open, respectful feedback and actually do something with it. Use 360-degree feedback tools, create regular feedback loops, and thank employees for speaking up. Feedback helps you grow, and responding well helps trust grow.

5. ***Be a Culture Creator, Not a Culture Cop.*** Instead of enforcing rules, model values. The best leaders don't just manage, they shape the tone, trust, and behaviors that define the workplace. When you consistently lead with empathy, you create a culture where people feel safe, respected, and inspired to do their best.

Leading with empathy is not about being soft. It's about being strong enough to understand what others need in order to succeed. When you tune into your people, you unlock performance, loyalty, and the untapped potential of your entire team.

"Baseball is a game of inches, and also a game of adjustments."

— Dusty Baker

6.

Learning Through Listening

Listening is one of those life skills that everyone assumes they're naturally good at like driving, parenting, or keeping a houseplant alive for more than a week. But just because you can hear doesn't mean you are actually listening. Yeah, I said it. And you've heard it before, too. Probably in a heated conversation where someone hit you with the classic: "I know you heard me, but were you listening?"

> *"Listening is one of those life skills that everyone assumes they're naturally good at—like driving, parenting, or keeping a houseplant alive for more than a week."*

It's a phrase as old as time, usually delivered with a look of disappointment, frustration, or both. And it stings because deep down, we know there's a difference between hearing and understanding words.

Listening is so fundamental that it's one of the first things doctors check in newborns. Ensuring they can react to sound. And yet, despite this early certification, many of us go on to become full-grown adults who are highly skilled at hearing noise but absolutely terrible at listening with intention.

It's not entirely our fault. We live in an era of constant noise, where our attention is pulled in more directions than a toddler in a toy store. Everywhere we turn, something is demanding our focus. According to various studies, the average person is bombarded with anywhere from 4,000 to 10,000 marketing messages daily. And thanks to the rise of digital advertising this number is only climbing.

With so much information fighting for space in our brains, it's no wonder we struggle to focus on what truly matters. Our minds have become expert multitaskers at the cost of deep, meaningful connections. And that's the problem. Because truly listening, especially between the lines, is the secret sauce to stronger relationships, better leadership, and, significantly fewer arguments that start with "That's not what I meant" and end with "Were you even listening?"

Let's do a quick exercise to prove just how hard it is to multitask, focus, and process the overwhelming amount of information thrown at us daily. Don't worry. This won't require heavy lifting, but fair warning: If you're in a public place, you might get a few weird looks.

Wherever you are—sitting, standing, or pretending to work—raise one arm and give a big ol' thumbs-up. Now, bring that thumb up to your eye level and lock your gaze on it. Really focus. Your thumb is now the most important thing in your world.

Now, keeping your thumb in position, shift your focus to something behind it. A picture on the wall, a coffee mug, or one of those always-empty hand sanitizer dispensers. Get that object in crystal-clear focus.

Now, switch back to your thumb. Then, back to the background object. Now, try to focus on both at the same time.

No matter how hard you try, your brain won't let you focus on both simultaneously. One will always come into sharp detail, while the other fades into a blur. It's not a flaw. It's just the way our brains are wired. Our minds are designed for selective attention, meaning we can truly focus on only one thing at a time.

This is exactly why texting and driving is so dangerous. In addition, we love to brag about our multitasking abilities, acting like we can answer emails, listen to a podcast, have a conversation, and meal prep all at once. The reality? We're just rapidly switching between tasks, giving partial attention to each. Meaning we are never fully present. It's also why, in conversations, we often "think" we're listening when we're actually just waiting for our turn to talk. We're hearing words, but we are not fully focused on them.

This exercise, or variations of it, has been widely used in mindfulness and attention training to highlight how multitasking is more of an illusion than a skill. In reality, we call "multitasking" just rapid task-switching, which reduces efficiency and focus. The same principle applies to listening. When we try to split our attention, we don't actually absorb everything being said. Instead, we catch fragments, miss nuances, and often respond to what we think we heard rather than what was actually communicated.

If you struggle to listen, don't beat yourself up. It's not just you. It's science. But if we want to build better relationships and become stronger leaders, we must train ourselves to stop splitting our focus and start listening with intention. Just like with focus exercises, we can develop better listening skills by intentionally eliminating distractions and truly tuning in to what's being said and what isn't.

What does it really mean to listen? And, more importantly, how can you get better at it? Think about how often you have nodded along in a conversation, pretending to absorb every word while secretly planning dinner or mentally reviewing your to-do list. (It's highly likely you are doing it right now, right?)

A quick Google search will tell you there are at least nine types of listening. Nine! And if you dare to go deeper into the abyss of the internet, you'll find dozens more, each one with a fancy name and a complicated definition. If you've ever sat through corporate workshops on "active listening" or "empathetic listening," you've probably smiled, nodded, and, ironically, stopped listening halfway through.

Listening isn't just about catching the words being said. It's about understanding what "isn't" being said. That's where true connection happens. If creating a positive culture is the foundation and leading with empathy is the framework, then listening—especially listening "between the lines"—is the glue that holds everything together.

The Difference
Between Hearing and Listening

If there's one thing that separates meaningful interactions from surface-level exchanges, it's emotional intelligence. At its core, emotional intelligence is the ability to understand, manage, and respond to emotions. Both your own and those of others. It's what allows people to navigate tough conversations, build trust, and create environments where others feel valued. Without it, even the best intentions fall flat because people don't engage with data and policies; they engage with emotions, relationships, and a sense of belonging.

Communication isn't just about words. It's a complex mix of tone, body language, and underlying emotions. Studies suggest that a significant portion of what we understand in a conversation comes not from the words themselves but from how they're said. A simple "I'm fine" can mean wildly different things depending on the tone, facial expression, and context. Yet, too often, we focus only on the words, missing the deeper message behind them. This is where true listening comes into play—not just processing sound but interpreting meaning.

Hearing and listening may seem like the same thing. Kind of like "replying" and "actually answering the question," but they couldn't be more different.

Hearing is like reading subtitles on mute. Listening is understanding the plot without them. Sure, you might catch a few words here and there, but without real engagement, you miss the meaning, the emotion, and the full context of what's happening.

> *"Hearing is like reading subtitles on mute. Listening is understanding the plot without them."*

In the workplace, this difference is painfully obvious. Ever had a boss who nodded along in a conversation but later acted like it never happened? That's because they heard you, but they weren't listening.

For example, an employee might say, "I've been feeling overwhelmed lately." A manager whose only hearing might respond with, "Got it. Let's push through!" Meanwhile, a listening manager would ask, "Tell me more. What's feeling unmanageable?" and actually take steps to address the concern.

Another situation often arises when an employee states, "I could really use some extra help on this project." The manager, hearing, not listening, possibly even looking at their cell phone, responds, "Yep, teamwork makes the dream work!" (And then does absolutely nothing.) However, a manager listening between the lines asks, "Do you feel like you're carrying too much of the load? Let's figure out a way to support you."

The key difference? Hearing is passive. Listening is active. Hearing lets sound in. Listening absorbs meaning. Want to be a better leader? It starts with conscious listening, not just to what's being said but to what's really being communicated.

It would be impossible to address the skill of listening without mentioning one of the most common strategies, Active Listening. The concept was first introduced by psychologists Carl R. Rogers and Richard E. Farson in their 1957 paper "Active Listening,"[16] where they emphasized that truly listening with sensitivity can foster personality change and stronger relationships. Their work laid the foundation for how we understand effective communication today. Later, Dr. Thomas Gordon built upon their research, popularizing Active Listening through his "Parent Effectiveness Training[17] programs in the 1960s, making them a practical tool for parents, educators, and leaders

---

16   https://wholebeinginstitute.com/wp-content/uploads/Rogers_Farson_Active-Listening.pdf

17   https://www.gordontraining.com/parenting/everything-need-know-active-listening

alike. The influence of Active Listening continues to shape leadership and interpersonal skills in workplaces and beyond.

Active Listening is at the heart of emotional intelligence. You cannot recognize emotions or respond to them effectively if you're not truly listening. Leaders who listen well can pick up on what's not being said. Reading between the lines of frustration, disengagement, or even unspoken enthusiasm. Emotional intelligence isn't just about knowing people's feelings; it's about hearing them. That's why Active Listening is more than just a communication tool. It's a leadership superpower.

Active Listening isn't just a leadership trend or soft skill to check off a list. It's a core competency that's taught in schools, professional training programs, and leadership-development courses across industries. From counseling to business to healthcare, professionals are trained to go beyond just hearing words—to pay attention to tone, emotion, hesitation, and even silence. Why? Because it works. Whether you're managing a team or meeting with a client, listening well builds trust, improves outcomes, and makes people feel seen. And in a workplace where most people just want to know they matter, that kind of listening becomes a real and measurable advantage.

Remember Mark, our manager from Chapter One? The one who meant well but missed the mark with his awkward team icebreaker? Had he taken a moment to truly listen to how his team responded—verbally and nonverbally—he might have picked up on the subtle (or not-so-subtle) signs that his approach wasn't resonating. Instead of assuming what engagement should look like, he could have asked for feedback, adjusted his strategy, and shown his team that their input actually mattered. That small act of listening could've built trust instead of quiet disengagement.

A simple shift, like allowing employees to share thoughts in a format that suits them or even kicking off the week with a quick wins-and-goals check-in instead of an icebreaker, could have made a world of difference. Active listening fosters trust and shows employees that their voices matter. A critical ingredient for a healthy workplace culture.

The lesson here? Culture isn't just built on activities. It's built on awareness. Mark wasn't wrong to want connection, but real engagement doesn't come from a one-size-fits-all approach. It comes from leaders who listen, adapt, and meet people where they are.

Listening Between the Lines

True listening goes beyond words. It's about recognizing tone, body language, and what isn't being said. People rarely communicate their full thoughts outright, whether out of discomfort, habit, or a fear of vulnerability. That's why effective listeners don't just hear words. They read the unspoken cues. As a professor of social work, I often share with the students to never trust what their client says. Yes, it seems counterintuitive, but in reality, most people don't know how to communicate their thoughts, ideas, and feelings effectively, due partly because of the social conditioning we experienced growing up.

Mark Scharenbroich, one of the all-time great professional speakers, shared a funny and relevant story in his video "The Greatest Days of Your Life (so far)."[18] Originally produced in 1984 by Jostens, this high school orientation film was written, performed, and directed by Scharenbroich himself. It quickly became a staple in schools nationwide, seen by millions of students throughout the mid-1980s. The film's humor and insightful message about the high school experience resonated so deeply that it earned both a "Golden Apple Film Award" and a "Silver Screen Industrial Film Award." Though it was created decades ago, the themes Scharenbroich explored, particularly the importance of connection, engagement, and the courage to ask questions, remain relevant today.

Mark Scharenbroich hilariously breaks down the sociological journey of a student from the eager, hand-waving elementary years to the silent, too-cool-for-questions high school experience.

It all starts in kindergarten through second grade, where students treat every question like a game show buzzer round. The teacher barely finishes asking, "Can anyone tell me—" before half the class jumps out of their seats, arms flailing, desperately hoping to be called on. Confidence? Through the roof. Fear of being wrong? Nonexistent.

But then, something shifts around third to fifth grade. A student gives an answer, and if it's wrong, the snickers start. A quiet "That was dumb," or a mumbled "Seriously?" from the peanut gallery suddenly introduces a new concept: judgment. For the first time, kids realize that their peers evaluate their answers. And just like that, the fearless enthusiasm of early childhood starts to dim.

---

18   https://www.youtube.com/watch?v=oE_icXuCdJg&ab_channel=Mark-Scharenbroich

By middle school, self-preservation kicks in. Raising your hand becomes a calculated risk. The safest bet? Staring at your desk, avoiding eye contact, and praying the teacher doesn't call your name.

And by the time students become high school seniors, the transformation is complete—raising a hand in class is no way uncool. Even if they know the answer, most won't dare volunteer it. Why? Because at this point, the fear of being judged, wrong, or—worst of all—teased has taken over.

Scharenbroich's story highlights a pattern we all recognize, one that doesn't just stop in the classroom. In many ways, what starts in grade school follows us into adulthood. People hesitate to speak up in meetings, share ideas, or take risks. Not because they don't have something valuable to contribute but because they've been conditioned from a young age to fear being wrong. And just like that, an entire room of intelligent, capable adults sits silently, waiting for someone else to raise their hand first.

And let's be honest, just like teens, adults don't want to be "that person." You know the one. The person who asks a question five minutes before the meeting is supposed to end. The one who speaks up when everyone else is already mentally halfway to lunch. That social pressure to stay quiet doesn't disappear when we grow up. It just shows up in conference rooms instead of classrooms.

And much like raising your hand in class, speaking up requires courage. Over time, silence becomes less of a choice and more of a defense mechanism rooted in fear. Fear of saying the wrong thing, of being judged, of making a comment that doesn't land well, or worse, being called out by a boss in front of everyone.

We learn this lesson early. As kids, we eagerly shared our thoughts—until the first time, we got an answer wrong and heard the quiet snickers or the dreaded "Seriously?" from a classmate. That moment stays with us. By the time we reach the workplace, many of us have been conditioned to hold back, calculating the risks of speaking up rather than engaging freely.

So we sit in meetings with something valuable to say but hesitate—because what if we're wrong? What if no one agrees? What if we sound foolish? And just like that, silence takes over. Not because we lack ideas or insight but because we've learned that avoiding discomfort feels safer than stepping into it.

Ironically, silence is also one of the most powerful tools in listening. But the difference between choosing silence and being silenced by fear determines the strength of our relationships and leadership. A well-placed pause in a conversation creates space for real thoughts to emerge. It allows people to say what they were holding back—what they really meant, not just what they initially felt safe offering. But if silence comes from a place of fear, it shuts down the connection before it even has a chance to begin.

This is where listening between the lines becomes crucial. Because not everyone will say exactly what they mean, and sometimes, the most important thing in the room isn't what's being said—it's what isn't. A classic example? "I'm fine." Anyone who's spent time coaching, managing, or in social work knows that fine is rarely fine. It's a placeholder, a shield, a socially acceptable way to dodge deeper discussion. Listening between the lines means noticing the hesitations, the forced smiles, and the shifts in tone. It means asking, "Are you sure?" at the right moment and creating the space for real conversations to unfold.

At the end of the day, the difference between being heard and being understood is the difference between noise and connection. And mastering that difference is what turns everyday conversations into opportunities for trust, insight, and real leadership.

How to Get Better at Listening

We all like to think we're good listeners. But in reality, most of us are just waiting for our turn to talk—or worse, mentally drafting our brilliant response while the other person is still speaking. The good news? Listening is a skill, not an innate talent, which means it can be improved with a little effort (and maybe some self-control).

One of the simplest ways to up your listening game is to pause before responding. Silence might feel awkward, but it's actually your best friend when it comes to absorbing what someone is saying. Instead of immediately blurting out your response, take a beat—just a few seconds—to let their words sink in. It shows you're actually processing instead of just waiting for your turn. Plus, it prevents you from accidentally cutting someone off mid-thought, which is a bonus if you don't want to be that person in conversations.

Another foolproof trick? Ask clarifying questions. How many times have you confidently nodded along in a conversation, only to realize later you had no clue what the person actually meant? Instead of assuming, try saying, "Tell me more about that?" or "Just to make sure I understand…" It's a simple way to avoid misinterpretations, and it spares you from that awkward moment when you confidently respond to something they never actually said.

Reflecting back on what you heard is another game-changer. Ever been in a conversation where you're pretty sure someone didn't hear a word you said? Don't be that person. A quick "So what you're saying is…" or "It sounds like you're feeling…" makes people feel heard and valued. It's like an instant credibility booster. Plus, it allows the speaker to correct you if you missed the mark.

If you really want to challenge yourself, try the three-second rule. And no, this isn't the one about dropping food on the floor (although, let's be honest, we all abide by that one, too). This rule says that after someone finishes speaking, you count to three in your head before responding. Why? Because it forces you to listen instead of jumping in immediately. It also gives the other person space to elaborate. Because sometimes, the most important things come after that initial pause.

And finally, let's talk about the urge to fix everything. We've all been guilty of going straight into "solution mode" the second someone shares a problem. But here's the thing—not everyone wants advice. Sometimes, people just need to vent without being handed a five-step action plan. A simple "Do you want advice, or do you just need to get it off your chest?" can work wonders. It saves you time, prevents unnecessary frustration, and, most importantly, makes the other person feel like their emotions matter more than just solving the problem at hand.

At the end of the day, becoming a better listener isn't about using fancy techniques or memorizing a script. It's about slowing down, staying present, and making sure the other person feels heard. And if all else fails, just remember—if you think you're a great listener, you probably still have room for improvement.

How Listening Between the Lines Improves Decision-Making

Good decision-making isn't just about having the right data—it's about understanding the situation. And that understanding doesn't just come from the words people say but from what they really mean. That's where listening between the lines becomes a game-changer.

When we actively listen—paying attention to tone, body language, and what isn't being said—we pick up on the deeper layers of a conversation. This insight is critical in decision-making because people don't always come right out and say what they mean. Sometimes, they downplay concerns, hesitate to express dissent or assume their emotions don't belong in the discussion. A leader who only hears the surface-level conversation may miss crucial details that impact the best course of action.

A good listener won't take their words at face value if a team member says, "I think we can meet that deadline," but their voice lacks confidence and avoids eye contact. They'll probe deeper. "It sounds like you have some concerns. What obstacles are you seeing?" That simple follow-up can uncover hidden issues, allowing for better planning, adjustments, or even a shift in strategy before problems arise.

Good listeners also know that this isn't the time to jump in with their own "I've been there too" moment. While sharing a personal story might feel helpful, it can unintentionally shift the focus away from the speaker and derail a valuable insight. Listening between the lines means holding space for someone else's experience without needing to match it with your own.

Better listening also helps leaders and professionals avoid reactive decision-making. When we only hear without truly listening, we risk making snap judgments based on partial information. But when we take the time to absorb what's really being communicated, we make more informed, thoughtful choices. Remember, reacting is based on emotion, while responding is based on thinking.

At its core, listening between the lines gives decision-makers a fuller picture that includes facts, emotions, logic, and intuition. And when decisions are made with a complete understanding of the situation, they're not just more effective they build trust, foster collaboration, and create solutions that truly address the needs of the people involved.

Why Listening Matters in Leadership

At its core, listening between the lines isn't just about communication—it's about trust. The ability to truly listen is what separates a leader people respect from one they simply report to. Employees, colleagues, and teams don't just want to be heard—they want to be understood. And when they feel understood, trust follows.

A leader who listens builds a culture where people feel valued. When employees' concerns, ideas, and even unspoken frustrations are recognized, they're more engaged, committed, and willing to bring their best selves to work. But when leaders only hear words without tuning into the deeper message, people quickly learn that their voices don't really matter. And nothing erodes trust faster than the feeling that speaking up is pointless.

> *"The difference between a great leader and an average one often comes down to this: Are you listening to respond, or are you listening to understand?"*

The difference between a great leader and an average one often comes down to this: Are you listening to respond, or are you listening to understand? One gathers information at face value. The other looks deeper, listening for patterns, unspoken concerns, and the real story behind the words. A leader who only listens for updates might miss early signs of burnout, disengagement, or brewing conflict. However, a leader who listens with curiosity and intention can identify issues before they become problems. That's not just better leadership. It's better decision-making, better culture, and better results.

When leaders practice listening between the lines, they foster a workplace where people feel safe, to be honest, to share ideas, and to voice concerns without fear of being dismissed. And that trust—the foundation of every strong relationship—is what turns a group of employees into a unified, committed team.

This is the 90% advantage. Most leaders focus on the loudest voices in the room. These are often the all-stars, the top performers, the most vocal contributors—even though they represent only a small portion of the team.

But the true strength of an organization lies in the everyday employees, the ones doing the quiet, consistent work that keeps everything running. They may not always speak up, but that doesn't mean they have nothing to say. The best leaders don't just listen to the 10% who command attention. They actively tune in to the 90% who often go unnoticed. Because when you listen between the lines, you don't just hear what's being said. You hear the potential waiting to be unlocked.

And in the end, listening isn't just a skill. It is leadership in action.

COPA AIRLINES – ELEVATING PERFORMANCE THROUGH ACTIVE LISTENING

Copa Airlines, headquartered in Panama, is renowned for its operational excellence and financial performance in the aviation industry. Despite this success, internal assessments revealed that while employee engagement was generally high, the company's leadership index—a key performance indicator reflecting leadership effectiveness—was not meeting desired benchmarks. This discrepancy indicated potential challenges in leadership communication and connection with employees.

Over a span of 15 months, Copa Airlines conducted extensive research, including over 50 focus groups with employees across various functions and levels. The findings highlighted a critical need for leaders to enhance their active listening and feedback skills. Employees expressed a desire for leaders who:

1. Listen and communicate frequently and respectfully.

2. Know their people and care about their well-being.

3. Guide, develop, and recognize their teams.

Recognizing the importance of these attributes, Copa Airlines sought a partnership to develop and implement a training program focused on these areas. Collaborating with the Center for Creative Leadership,[19] Copa Airlines introduced a half-day workshop centered on effective feedback and active listening. The training emphasized the Situation-Behavior-Impact™ feedback model and techniques to enhance active listening, enabling leaders to fully understand and engage with their teams. A train-the-trainer approach was adopted to ensure scalability and sustainability, empowering over 20 vice presidents and directors to facilitate the workshops internally. This strategy allowed Copa to reach more than 1,000 leaders within a year.

Post-training assessments demonstrated significant improvements:

1. Organizational Climate: Increased from 72% to 78%.

2. Engagement: Rose from 75% to 82%.

3. Leadership Index: Improved from 67% to 70%.

These metrics reflect a more connected and communicative leadership team, leading to enhanced employee satisfaction and organizational performance. The initiative underscored the value of active listening and effective feedback in fostering a positive workplace culture.

Copa Airlines' commitment to refining leadership behaviors through focused training on active listening and feedback has improved key performance indicators and strengthened the overall organizational culture. This case exemplifies how targeted development programs can address specific challenges, leading to measurable improve-

---

19   https://www.ccl.org/client-successes/case-studies/helping-leaders-form-deeper-connections-by-building-active-listening-feedback-skills/

ments in both leadership effectiveness and employee engagement.

Copa Airlines didn't just hold a few workshops and hope for the best. They made intentional, organization-wide moves that turned insight into action. Here are three lessons worth stealing—uh, modeling—from their success:

1. **Make Listening a Leadership Priority** – Copa realized that listening wasn't just a soft skill but a performance lever. By making active listening and feedback central to leadership development, they elevated both engagement and effectiveness across the company.

2. **Scale with Sustainability in Mind** – Instead of relying solely on outside facilitators, they trained their own leaders to deliver the program internally. This built internal capability and created buy-in from the top down. When VPs are the ones leading the learning, people tend to pay attention.

3. **Connect Listening to Outcomes** – They measured results—and the numbers spoke loudly. Increases in employee engagement, organizational climate, and their leadership index weren't just a nice bonus. They were direct results of leaders learning to hear not just what was said but what was meant.

Copa's story proves what we've been saying all along: When leaders take the time to truly listen and listen between the lines, everyone wins. It's not about perfect messaging or polished communication. It's about presence. It's about paying attention to what's said, hinted at, and left unsaid.

Copa didn't just improve engagement scores. They shifted the way their leaders show up. By building the skill of active listening, they created space for trust, clarity, and real connection—things every team craves but not every leader delivers.

Because the truth is, the most powerful thing a leader can do isn't to give the best speech. It's asking the right question and listening as if the answer matters. When you tune in to the people who aren't always speaking the loudest, you uncover the insight, effort, and potential that have been there all along.

And that's the 90% advantage.

LISTENING BETWEEN THE LINES

Here are five actionable ways to upgrade your listening from passive hearing to powerful connection, because real leadership begins the moment you stop talking.

1. ***Slow Down to Speed Up. Don't race to reply.*** A few seconds of silence might feel uncomfortable, but it creates space for others to elaborate—and for you to absorb what's really being said. Practicing the "three-second rule" before responding helps you hear both the message and the meaning behind it.

2. ***Ask, Don't Assume.*** If you catch yourself nodding without really understanding, pause and ask clarifying questions. "Can you say more about that?" or "What would support look like for you right now?" opens doors to honesty and avoids dangerous misinterpretations.

3. ***Read the Room, Not Just the Words.*** Tone, body language, hesitation, and even silence carry as much information as dialogue. "I'm fine" rarely means "I'm fine." Listen for what's missing and gently dig deeper when something feels off. Trust your gut—then verify with curiosity.

4. ***Reflect and Reframe.*** Practice paraphrasing to confirm understanding. "So what I'm hearing is…" or "It sounds like you're feeling…" validates the speaker and builds immediate trust. It also lets them

clarify if you missed the mark, which happens to the best of us.

5. ***Hold Space Before You Solve.*** Sometimes people don't want solutions. They want support. Before you dive into fix-it mode, ask: "Do you want help working through this or do you just need me to listen?" Respecting the difference shows emotional intelligence and strengthens relationships.

When you listen between the lines, you don't just gather information—you build connection, uncover insight, and unlock the kind of potential that most leaders overlook. Listening isn't a soft skill. It's a strategic advantage.

CORE PRINCIPLE III

Strengthening Resiliency Through Adversity

"Sometimes we need to feel lost to find out who we really are."

— Joy in *Inside Out 2*

7.

Bouncing Back With Purpose

One of the most iconic and prolific singer-songwriters of our time is none other than Billy Joel. And yes, my wife and I enjoyed attending one of his legendary Madison Square Garden concerts in December 2019. As a lifelong fan, it was a true bucket-list moment, and it did not disappoint. Among his countless hits, one song that continues to resonate with people across generations is "Pressure," the biggest single off his eighth studio album, The Nylon Curtain, released in 1982.

If you're a fan of his music, you might remember the lyrics:

> You have to learn to pace yourself
> Pressure
> You're just like everybody else
> Pressure

Joel spoke about its inspiration and meaning shortly after the song's release. Surprisingly, it wasn't the high-stakes music industry pressure he was writing about. It was something much more relatable. "The pressure I was writing about in this song wasn't necessarily music-business pressure," Joel revealed in an interview. "It was writing pressure." As it turns out, "Pressure" was born from his own creative struggles while working on the album. Halfway through recording, he hit a wall. "I didn't have any ideas.

I thought, 'It's gone, it's dead, I have nothing. Nothing. Nothing,'" Joel admitted.

And then, as fate would have it, inspiration walked through the door in the form of his secretary. Seeing his frustration, she casually remarked, "Wow, you look like you're under a lot of pressure. I bet that'd be a good idea for a song." And just like that, lightning struck. "Thank you," Joel recalled thinking. And the rest, as they say, is history.

Pressure is as much a part of life as morning coffee and Wi-Fi passwords you can't remember. We all experience it in different ways, and if you're like most people, you've developed a personal arsenal of coping mechanisms to deal with it. Some of the healthiest ways to channel stress include exercising, journaling, meditating, reading, or engaging in hobbies that don't involve doom-scrolling through social media at 2 a.m. These activities help us stay sane and prevent us from turning into human pressure cookers ready to blow at any moment.

But pressure comes at us from all angles, like an overly enthusiastic personal trainer shouting, "You can do more!" There's the pressure to succeed and pay the bills; let's not forget the pressure to make money. Because, apparently, that's important. Then there's the pressure from your spouse who wants you to remember "that thing" they told you about last week, the pressure from your kids who somehow think you're an endless source of snacks and wisdom, and the pressure of keeping your boss happy while pretending you have everything under control. Pressure, pressure, pressure. It's lurking around every corner, hiding in every email, and waiting for you at the grocery store self-checkout when the machine inevitably malfunctions.

Somewhere in the past twenty years, I stumbled upon a website called Simple Truths. They offer an array of business motivation and personal inspiration books and videos, perfect for those moments when you need a quick boost of wisdom without sitting through another three-hour webinar. Over time, the site evolved, but one video stuck with me, and I've repeatedly used it with my clients. It was called 212°: The Extra Degree, based on the motivational book by Mac Anderson and Sam Parker.[20]

The premise of 212° is deceptively simple but incredibly powerful. Water boils at exactly 212 degrees Fahrenheit. At that moment, something amazing happens. Water doesn't just get hotter; it transforms. It goes from a simmering liquid to a force of nature, producing steam. And what's so special about steam? It's the powerhouse behind steam engines, capable of moving massive trains and carrying them across vast distances. All it takes is "one extra degree" to create enough pressure to push forward and spark real movement. The metaphor here practically writes itself. When harnessed correctly, pressure doesn't just make us sweat. It fuels us to accomplish incredible things.

Pressure has the power to turn stagnant water into an unstoppable force. What if we looked at the pressures in our own lives the same way? Instead of viewing pressure as an overwhelming weight pressing down on us, what if we saw it as the energy source that propels us forward? Whether it's work deadlines, financial responsibilities, or simply juggling a never-ending to-do list, the pressure we face can either weigh us down or push us to that next level. Our own personal steam engine is ready to take off.

20 https://www.simpletruths.com/personal-inspiration/ignite-reads-212-the-extra-degree.html

The truth is that pressure is unavoidable. It lurks in our inboxes, calendars, and even our families (especially when someone asks, "What's for dinner?" for the third time in an hour). But here's the good news. You're not alone in the struggle. Everyone experiences pressure, from world-famous musicians feeling the heat to meet expectations to the rest of us just trying to stay afloat. The key isn't avoiding pressure but figuring out how to turn it into fuel rather than frustration.

Whether it's hitting the gym, diving into a great book, or sneaking five minutes of solitude behind a locked bathroom door (no judgment), learning how to channel pressure is crucial. Once you figure out how to manage it, whether through self-care, goal-setting, or sheer determination, you can harness that energy and turn it into progress.

So, the next time you feel like you're about to boil over, remember: You're just one degree away from making steam. And with that, who knows? You might just be the engine that drives your own success story.

There Are No Mistakes

Some of the most common fears that keep people up at night—right after the fear of accidentally hitting "Reply All"—include the fear of public speaking, the fear of the unknown, and the ever-classic fear of failure or making mistakes. Sure, humans have hundreds, if not thousands, of fears. Some are perfectly rational, like the fear of heights (because gravity is real), while others are, let's say, more "creative," like the fear of clowns or the fear of running out of Wi-Fi at a crucial moment. But when it comes to personal and professional growth, the heavyweight champion of fears is undoubtedly the fear of failure. And what leads to failure? Mistakes. And failure and mistakes are another form of pressure we deal with daily.

This pressure, often stemming from fear of mistakes, is particularly detrimental to the 90% of employees who quietly carry the weight of an organization. It reinforces a mindset of perfectionism and avoidance, stifling creativity and risk-taking. The 90% advantage shifts the focus, recognizing that sustainable success doesn't come from avoiding failure but from using mistakes as opportunities to grow and improve. Leaders who adopt this perspective empower their teams to see setbacks as valuable lessons rather than career-ending catastrophes.

Our entire academic journey revolves around avoiding the dreaded "F." Because F doesn't stand for Fantastic or Fearless; nope, it's FAIL, plain and simple. Now, take a step back and ask, how outdated is this system? If F equals Fail, then what does an A stand for? Oh, right—Awesome! And B? Uh…Better than average? Maybe barely impressive? And then there's C, which obviously stands for Craptastic because, let's be honest, nobody brags about a C. Then we have D, which most people automatically translate to Dumb.

Somewhere along the way, schools completely ditched the letter E. Why? Everyone knows E stands for Excellent, and we simply cannot have Excellent awkwardly sandwiched between Dumb and Fail. It would throw off the whole system! So, instead of rethinking the scale, they just removed E entirely, leaving us all to grow up thinking anything less than an A is a one-way ticket to Loserville.

This system drilled into us from an early age tells us that mistakes are bad, setbacks are shameful, and perfection is the only acceptable outcome. No wonder the fear of mistakes resonates so deeply when I speak to a room full of athletes. Mistakes aren't just momentary slip-ups in their world—they're ticking time bombs. Mistakes lead to errors. Errors lead to losses. Then that leads to a symphony of frustration from teammates, coaches, and parents, and let's not forget the ever-so-helpful armchair quarterbacks in the stands who suddenly become experts on everything you did wrong.

But wait, there's more! Losing isn't just emotionally painful; coaches often throw in something extra to drive the lesson home: punishment. And what's the universal punishment in sports? That's right—running. Lots and lots of running. Somehow, coaches believe that sprinting suicides after a loss will magically transform you into a better player. And if running isn't enough, there's always the dreaded alternative: the bench. Nothing strikes fear into an athlete's heart like the words, "If you don't start playing, you'll be watching from the bench."

And that's where things get tricky. If losing equals punishment, and punishment equals the bench, then what message does that send to the poor souls already sitting there? If the bench is bad, does that mean I'm bad? Am I not a real part of the team? Suddenly, the bench isn't just a place to catch your breath—it's a scarlet letter branding you as irrelevant, useless, and the human embodiment of failure.

Let's dive into the mental gymnastics that happen when you run laps of shame after a loss. First, the self-blame kicks in: "I can't believe I missed that shot. I suck." Then, as the sweat drips and the lungs burn, frustration turns outward:

"Why is Coach making us run? I didn't try to lose! Does he think I enjoy screwing up? What an ass!" And finally, the pièce de résistance: anger shifts to your teammates. Not the ones who hustled, no, no. The ones who made the mistakes that "cost" you the game. Suddenly, the locker room turns into a battleground. Fueled by frustration, you march in and unload on your teammate: "Thanks a lot for making me run. Maybe next time you'll actually show up."

And just like that, a loss turns into finger-pointing, resentment, and disconnection. Does that sound like a team you'd want to be a part of? Of course not. Because here's the truth: Nobody likes losing. No one steps onto the field or court thinking, "Let's really tank this one." Everyone is doing their best, but when fear takes over, it poisons the things that make sports great: teamwork, resilience, and growth.

The doom doesn't end in the locker room. It's just getting started. Like a dark cloud, it follows you as you trudge out and spot your parents waiting. You brace yourself, hop in the car, and within seconds—bam—you get rear-ended, not by another vehicle but by the inevitable post-game analysis, delivered precisely by a sports commentator who's been studying your every move since kindergarten. It doesn't matter if you played halfway decent or even had a few highlight moments. Your folks are ready to break it all down like they're on ESPN.

Welcome to the wonderful tradition of post-game parental feedback, something you've endured since you first stepped onto a field as a wide-eyed five-year-old in an oversized jersey. The car ride home becomes a greatest hit album of criticisms, negative comments, and subtle (or not-so-subtle) threats about how you "better step it up" or else. And let's not forget the icing on the cake. The mass disappointment in their voices, carefully sprinkled with sighs, head shakes, and the dreaded, "I just don't understand what happened out there."

Is it any wonder why we fear mistakes, failure, and losing? When the people we love the most, the ones whose approval we crave, become the harshest critics, reinforcing every doubt we already had bubbling inside. Instead of building us up, they remind us, in vivid detail, of every missed opportunity, every poor decision, and why we might never be as good as we hoped. They mean well. They think they're "helping." But in reality, they're only cementing the belief that mistakes are unacceptable, failure is shameful, and losing is the ultimate disgrace. No pressure, right? And once again, there's that word "pressure."

At some point in your life, whether it was a well-meaning parent, a patient teacher, or even an oddly enthusiastic boss, you've probably heard them say, "I want you to make mistakes." Yep, they said it, straight to your face, with a smile even. And let's be honest, your first thought was probably, "Are you serious? Why would anyone want me to mess up?" But they weren't secretly rooting for your downfall. They knew something you didn't: Mistakes are where the real learning happens.

But when exactly does a mistake become a mistake? Do you wake up in the morning with a cup of coffee and say, "Today is the day! I can't wait to make some epic mistakes." Uh, no. And when you have a huge project due, do you eagerly anticipate messing it up just for the life lesson? Absolutely not. Mistakes are sneaky little things. You only realize you've made one after the fact. You don't say, "I'm making a mistake," you say, "I made a mistake." See what happened there? Past tense. The reality is that mistakes are only mistakes when we look back at them and slap a label on the experience.

And let's talk about that label. Over time, we've been conditioned to believe that mistakes are bad. Something to be avoided at all costs. We get frustrated, embarrassed, and sometimes downright angry when we slip up. But what if we've been looking at mistakes all wrong? What if, instead of seeing them as failures, we saw them as "progress in camouflage?" If every mistake teaches us something valuable, then technically, they aren't mistakes. They are learning opportunities in disguise.

Every successful person you admire has made their fair share of mistakes, whether it's an entrepreneur, athlete, or even that one person at work who always seems to have it together. The difference? They don't see mistakes as stop signs. They see them as annoying speed bumps but nothing that brings the whole journey to a halt. It's time to rethink how we view mistakes. They are not something to be punished but opportunities to learn and improve. Mistakes aren't just inevitable; they're essential. They prove that you're trying, pushing boundaries, and stepping outside your comfort zone.

> *"Every successful person you admire has made their fair share of mistakes, whether it's an entrepreneur, athlete, or even that one person at work who always seems to have it together."*

Unfortunately, they don't teach in school that failure isn't the end of the road. In fact, as we have seen, it is just the opposite. Yet, it's often the only way to learn, grow, and eventually succeed. It's time to stop fearing the F and start embracing the idea that sometimes, failure is the best teacher we never knew we needed. Mistakes and failure aren't the enemy. They are not some lurking villains waiting to ruin your career, relationships, or perfectly curated social media personas. They are your personal, often painful, growth consultants.

That's the heart of the 90% advantage. It's not about chasing flawless performance or idolizing the top 10%. It's about empowering the everyday players, the reliable contributors, the ones who show up, try hard, and, yes, occasionally mess up. The 90% don't want to make mistakes. So don't punish them when they do. Instead, ask them what they learned. Ask what they'll do differently next time because that conversation builds trust, not fear.

And while we may not send employees to run laps after a loss, we do bench them. We pull them off the important project. We pass them over for promotions. We withhold raises or bonuses—quietly reinforcing the message that mistakes equal irrelevance. But that's not leading. That's control. And it kills growth.

Leaders who want to unlock potential can't just tolerate mistakes. They have to normalize them. Create a culture where slip-ups aren't seen as signs of weakness but as signals of engagement. When the 90% stop fearing failure, they start stepping up. They get braver, bolder, and better. That's the real advantage.

So don't fear failure. Embrace it. Laugh at it, learn from it, and recognize it for what it truly is: a necessary pit stop on the road to success. Adjust your perspective and turn mistakes into milestones. When you shift your mindset, you'll realize something profound. There are no mistakes, only opportunities—and in the grand scheme of things, the only real failure is letting the fear of failure stop you from even trying.

Mastering the Powers of Motivation

Motivation becomes very real when you're staring down a bear or when a snake decides to make itself comfortable near your feet. At that moment, you have exactly two choices: run for your life (extrinsic motivation) or take a deep breath, channel your inner survivalist, and figure out your next move (intrinsic motivation). The bear or snake isn't pausing to give you time to weigh your options. They are right there, and it's up to you to act fast. Whether you choose to sprint like an Olympic athlete or rely on your instincts and training to maneuver the situation, motivation is the driving force behind survival. Believe it or not, the workplace isn't all that different. Every day presents unexpected challenges—tight deadlines, demanding clients, and those sudden "We need this done yesterday" emails that feel just as alarming as spotting a bear in the wild.

> *"Motivation is a lot like surviving in the wilderness. Some people have an internal compass and fire-starting skills, while others need a map, a flare gun, and a well-stocked survival kit."*

Motivation is a lot like surviving in the wilderness. Some people have an internal compass and fire-starting skills (intrinsic motivation), while others need a map, a flare gun, and a well-stocked survival kit (extrinsic motivation). In the workplace, both types are essential for navigating the daily challenges and unexpected obstacles that come with the territory. Intrinsic motivation is the inner drive that keeps you going, even when no one's watching— it's the satisfaction of solving a tough problem, mastering a new skill, or simply taking pride in a job well done, much like building a fire from scratch. On the other hand, extrinsic motivation is a much-needed external boost, whether it's a paycheck, a promotion, or a celebratory team lunch that feels like finding an unexpected stash of granola bars in your backpack.

In the business world, leaders play the role of survival guides, tasked with figuring out who's the rugged, self-sufficient type and who needs a little extra guidance to stay on track. Some employees will blaze their own trail with purpose and passion, while others might need a skilled trail guide to keep moving forward. Just like in the wild, the workplace is full of unforeseen challenges. Tight deadlines, shifting goals, and those "urgent" emails that pop up like sudden thunderstorms. The difference? In the office, you can't always outrun the problem. Whether it's dealing with a tough project or managing workplace drama, your motivation—whether driven by external pressures or internal ambition—dictates how you respond and, ultimately, how well you survive the daily grind. The key for leaders is knowing when to let someone trek ahead independently and when to step in with a metaphorical compass and some well-timed encouragement.

A perfect example that beautifully illustrates the difference between intrinsic and extrinsic motivation is the classic movie, The Karate Kid. Whether you were captivated by the original in the '80s or got hooked by the modern reboot, the story offers a timeless lesson in how motivation shapes success, personal growth, and resilience. It's a tale that resonates across generations, showing us that the drive to achieve can come from within or be fueled by external pressures and how the source of that motivation can ultimately determine our long-term fulfillment and success.

Daniel LaRusso is the underdog hero of the story. Initially, his motivation to learn karate comes from an external need to defend himself from bullies. But as he trains under the wise and patient Mr. Miyagi, something shifts. Daniel realizes that karate isn't just about fighting; it's about self-discipline, confidence, and personal growth. His motivation evolves from seeking protection to pursuing mastery for its own sake. This is intrinsic motivation at its best. He finds fulfillment in the process, the improvement, and the deeper philosophy behind the art rather than just focusing on winning the big tournament.

On the flip side, we have Johnny Lawrence and the Cobra Kai dojo. Their approach to karate is almost entirely driven by extrinsic motivation. They train for the trophies, the recognition, and the approval of their intense and demanding sensei, who preaches the infamous "no mercy" mantra. For Johnny and his teammates, success is defined by external validation. It's all about winning at all costs, gaining status, and avoiding failure. They're fueled by pressure and expectations rather than a genuine love for the craft.

Ultimately, the contrast between Daniel and Cobra Kai highlights a critical lesson. Intrinsic motivation leads to sustainable success, growth, and resilience. Extrinsic motivation, if not balanced, can result in burnout, fear of failure, and a shallow sense of achievement. Daniel's journey teaches us that true progress comes from within. At the same time, Johnny's story reminds us that relying solely on external rewards can leave us feeling empty once the competition ends.

Whether in karate, business, or life, The Karate Kid teaches us that true success isn't just about collecting awards, promotions, or hitting quarterly targets. It's about aligning your efforts with a clear purpose, driving meaningful impact, and finding satisfaction in the work itself. External rewards like bonuses and recognition can provide a temporary boost. However, the internal drive, whether it's our commitment to growth, resilience, and continuous improvement, creates lasting success. This lesson is more important than ever in the corporate world, where pressure to perform often overshadows personal development.

Just like Daniel LaRusso faced Cobra Kai, professionals encounter fierce competition, demanding expectations, and relentless pressure to stay ahead. But real achievement comes not from quick wins or external validation but from mastering the art of perseverance, focusing on what's within our control, and consistently working toward long-term goals. the 90% advantage leverages the steady, intrinsic motivation of the majority of your workforce. The everyday performers who, with the right leadership and support, can transform themselves and your organization. Success isn't just about milestones; it's about continuous growth, learning, and development. So, whether you're navigating boardrooms or bottom lines, remember that sustainable success is built one motivated step at a time.

So, how does a leader help build that kind of internal drive? Start by creating an environment where effort is noticed, not just outcomes. Ask meaningful questions like, "What part of this work energizes you?" or "What skill do you want to develop next?" Recognize growth, not just results. Let your team set some of their own goals and give them space to experiment—even fail—without fear. Give them challenges that stretch their skills, and then cheer for the progress, not just the finish line. When people feel ownership over their work, when they see how their role connects to something bigger, they stop working for rewards and start working with purpose. That's how you light the fire from within—and that's the spark that fuels the 90% advantage.

A CASE STUDY

MARVEL RISING FROM BANKRUPTCY TO SUPERHERO STARDOM[21]

In the early 1990s, Marvel Comics was riding high as one of the comic book industry's most influential and recognizable brands. With iconic characters like Spider-Man, the X-Men, and the Avengers, the company seemed unstoppable. However, by 1996, Marvel found itself in a financial crisis, ultimately filing for bankruptcy. Oversaturation of the market reliance on gimmicky collectible sales and poor management decisions left the company struggling to survive. What once was a thriving empire now faced the very real possibility of fading into obscurity.

Instead of accepting defeat, Marvel's leadership saw an opportunity to reinvent the company in a bold and unexpected way. They decided to pivot from their traditional comic book focus and venture into the film industry. While previous attempts at Marvel-based movies had seen mixed success, this time, they were determined to take full creative control. By emphasizing quality storytelling, character-driven narratives, and staying true to their comic book roots, Marvel aimed to bring their superheroes to life on the big screen like never before.

What truly set Marvel apart during this transition was their intrinsic motivation. A deep-seated passion for storytelling and a belief in the power of their characters to

---

21 https://www.webfx.com/blog/marketing/how-5-big-brands-came-back-from-the-brink-of-failure/

inspire audiences. They understood that true success wasn't just about making money but about creating meaningful connections through their stories. With this mindset, they took a major leap of faith in 2008 with the release of Iron Man, the first installment of what would become the Marvel Cinematic Universe (MCU). The film's success validated their strategy, and Marvel found itself on a new trajectory toward unprecedented success.

Over the next decade, the MCU became a cultural and financial powerhouse, with films like The Avengers and Black Panther breaking box office records and reshaping the entertainment industry. Marvel recovered from their financial mistakes and set a new storytelling, branding, and fan engagement standard. Their journey from near collapse to becoming one of the most successful entertainment franchises in history is a testament to the power of perseverance, adaptability, and staying true to one's core values.

Here are the key lessons from Marvel's comeback:

1. ***Adaptability is Essential for Survival:*** Marvel's ability to pivot from comic books to film proved that embracing change and taking calculated risks can turn failure into opportunity.

2. ***Intrinsic Motivation Drives Long-Term Success:*** Their deep passion for storytelling and belief in their characters fueled their determination and led to the creation of an entertainment empire.

3. ***Mistakes Are Opportunities in Disguise:*** Marvel's financial struggles forced them to rethink their approach and ultimately paved the way for a more innovative and resilient company.

Marvel's story is a powerful reminder that setbacks are not the end but opportunities to reassess, refocus, and emerge stronger than ever.

BOUNCING BACK WITH PURPOSE

Great leaders aren't the ones who avoid pressure. They're the ones who turn it into power. Here's how to help your team bounce back—not just with grit, but with purpose.

1. ***Normalize the Pressure,*** Don't Pretend It's Not There. Pressure isn't going anywhere. Acknowledge it openly. When leaders name the elephant in the room, it reduces anxiety and builds trust. Say things like, "We're in a crunch, but we've got the talent to handle this," or "Yes, this is a stretch—but it's also a chance to level up."

2. ***Reframe Mistakes as Momentum.*** The next time someone on your team drops the ball, don't lead with "what went wrong?" Instead, try "What did we learn?" Treat mistakes like data—feedback, not failure. When you do, you build a culture where risk-taking and innovation thrive. As Billy Joel might say, give them permission to find inspiration in the pressure.

3. ***Fuel the Fire with Intrinsic Motivation.*** Everyone loves a bonus, but long-term performance doesn't come from trophies—it comes from purpose. Help employees connect the dots between their tasks and the bigger picture. Ask: "What excites you about this project?" or "How does this work tap into your strengths?" You're not just managing performance— you're unlocking passion.

4. ***Let the 90% take the shot***. Stop giving every stretch assignment to the top 10%. Instead, look to the steady contributors who've been showing up, doing the work, and waiting for their moment. Offer them a challenge, back them up, and make it clear: Mistakes won't get them benched—growth will get them noticed.

5. ***Bounce Back Publicly, Not Just Privately***. When the team rebounds from a setback, don't just debrief behind closed doors. Celebrate the comeback. Tell the story of how they adapted, learned, and improved. It turns failure into folklore and shows everyone that pressure isn't something to fear.
It's something to rise through. Pressure can crack foundations or forge something unbreakable. When leaders create space for recovery, growth, and motivation, they don't just reduce burnout. They build a culture of courage. And that's what turns the everyday into extraordinary.

"When life gets you down, you know what you gotta do? Just keep swimming."

— Dory in *Finding Nemo*

8.

But Can You Pitch

In the sports arena, when an athlete gets banged up, you often hear the familiar rallying cries: "Rub some dirt in it," "We've got ice," and the ever-popular "Shake it off!" While these expressions might seem like mere clichés, they actually capture a powerful lesson in resiliency. One that is just as essential in the boardroom as it is on the playing field.

For the past 15 years, I've navigated the wild world of youth softball as a proud (and sometimes exasperated) parent of two talented pitchers. The older of the two, a now former high school standout in New Jersey who racked up All-Conference and All-County honors, chose not to pursue college play. Meanwhile, my youngest daughter is busy sharpening her pitching and hitting skills under the tutelage of a dedicated pitching and hitting coach.

Let me take you back to a memorable day in the fall of 2021. My daughter, the leadoff hitter and our starting pitcher, was at bat when a ball ricocheted off her bat and smacked her finger. Tears streaming down her face, she called time and insisted on an immediate trip to the ER. As a concerned—and perhaps overly optimistic—father coaching her fall softball team, I tried to reassure her: "Don't worry, it's just a blood blister. You're fine. Just finish the at-bat." She pushed through only to request another ER visit. Again, I downplayed it: "I swear, it's just a blood blister. You're fine." She took herself out of the game, exclaiming how much it hurt. After realizing her attempts to gain my attention fell on deaf ears, she called her mom. I even had her show it to the assistant coach, who quickly offered his "professional" medical opinion that it was indeed a blood blister and to just "put some ice on it."

Meanwhile, at my youngest daughter's game, my wife was on hand to support her. Upon receiving the urgent call from her oldest daughter, she left that game and picked her up to take her to the ER. When she arrived, I maintained my trademark nonchalance, advising, "Put some ice on it. She'll be fine."

After the game, my cell phone rang as I was heading back to my car. It was my daughter. I answered, slightly annoyed, "So, a blood blister, right?" Her voice, filled with disbelief and pain, shot back, "No, it's broken in three places. I told you so!" In the background, I could almost hear my wife fuming at my dismissive attitude toward what was clearly a significant injury. Yet, in that stunned moment, I couldn't resist asking, "But can you pitch?" I meant every word—especially with another game in two days—and I desperately didn't want to believe I was that bad of a dad.

The very next day at the orthopedic doctor's office, the grim reality was confirmed. Her break was severe enough to sideline her for the rest of the fall season and most of the winter. Whenever she reminded me that her injury wasn't just a simple blood blister, I would ask my trademark question: "But can you pitch?"

After my daughter's finger healed and she bounced back with a fantastic spring season, another situation arose with my youngest two years later. During tryouts, she caught a fly ball that hit the ring finger of her throwing hand. When she got home and showed me the injury, I couldn't help but ask again, though this time, I was completely serious: "Can you pitch?"

She grabbed a ball, squeezed it, and confidently replied, "Yes." Even though her finger turned black and blue and swelled up, she never mentioned any pain or thought about seeing a doctor. Whenever I asked if she could pitch, she answered a simple, unwavering "Yes." Remarkably, she not only finished the season—pitching for both the freshman and JV teams to secure a 15–4 record with nearly 75 strikeouts—but she also showcased her resilience. A week after the season ended, we took her for a routine check-up with our orthopedic doctor, who quickly confirmed that her finger was indeed broken, though it was already healing and left slightly crooked for life. We exchanged smiles and, with a shared sense of defiance, she said, "But, I could pitch."

Just when the saga seemed to be over, a twist arrived while playing volleyball during gym class in the winter during the following school year. A spiked ball smashed into her hand, targeting that same infamous ring finger. This time, I donned my responsible parent hat and took her to the doctor within 24 hours. An X-ray revealed not only a fracture but also a pulled tendon, which meant a mandatory four-week benching to ensure proper healing. I braced for the tough news but understood that these challenges were invaluable life lessons, even if she wasn't exactly thrilled. And, adding a final dash of humor to the ordeal, when she told her boyfriend her finger was in a splint, his first question was, "But, can you pitch?"

Looking back, those well-intentioned parental pep talks and classic sports banter turned a routine injury into an enduring lesson in resilience. Today, whenever something's off, I call it a "blood blister." A gentle reminder that it's not the end of the world. And then I always follow up with, "Yeah, but can you pitch?" It's more than just a lighthearted phrase. It's become a reminder to face challenges head-on, demonstrate resilience, and always ask ourselves if we're ready to keep moving forward, no matter the setback. Just like my daughters, who have persevered time and again, this question serves as a mantra for navigating those inevitable obstacles life throws at all of us.

Everyday Game Changers: Harnessing Resilience to Master the Comeback

In sports, the true game changers aren't always the flashy superstars—they're the resilient ones who bounce back from adversity with the tenacity of a well-worn bouncy ball. Consider Wayne Gretzky's relentless drive, Tom Brady's clutch performances, or Serena Williams's unwavering spirit. These athletes prove that setbacks aren't the final whistle but rather a chance to reset the play. In fact, research by Fletcher and Sarkar (2012[22]) highlights that elite athletes often harness resilience to transform adversity into opportunity.

> *"In sports, the true game changers aren't always the flashy superstars—they're the resilient ones who bounce back from adversity with the tenacity of a well-worn bouncy ball."*

22 Fletcher, D., & Sarkar, M. (2012). A grounded theory of psychological resilience in Olympic champions. Psychology of Sport and Exercise, 13(5), 669–678.

Just as field goals often go unnoticed until they clinch the win, those everyday recoveries—those moments when you dust yourself off and even share a laugh over a misstep—form the backbone of any winning team. These small victories, these micro-moments of resilience, remind us that adversity isn't a dead end; it's the setup for a remarkable comeback. When we embrace the humorous, human side of "shaking off" life's mishaps, we fuel our intrinsic motivation and tackle external challenges head-on. True game changers are born in these uncelebrated moments, ready to redefine victory one resilient play at a time.

Who doesn't love the comeback story? One of the most iconic examples is Colonel Harland Sanders, the man behind KFC. In his mid-60s—when most of us would consider settling into retirement—Sanders faced rejection after rejection, reportedly being turned down over a thousand times before someone finally embraced his secret chicken recipe. His unwavering determination transformed a string of setbacks into a global phenomenon. Much like the 90% of us who overcome daily challenges, Sanders's journey shows that resilience isn't reserved for the superstars—it's the everyday hero's secret sauce. His story reminds us that every setback is simply the prelude to a winning comeback, no matter how fried it may seem.

Another iconic comeback story comes from J.K. Rowling, the mastermind behind the Harry Potter series. Before enchanting the world with magic, Rowling was a struggling single mother battling poverty and depression. Imagine being rejected by 12 different publishing houses for Harry Potter and the Sorcerer's Stone—yet she refused to hang up her wand. Instead, she turned every setback into a stepping stone, harnessing the power of everyday victories to fuel her relentless drive.

Rowling's journey isn't about instant magical fame; it's a testament to the 90% of us who face daily challenges and choose to rise above them. After finally being embraced by Bloomsbury, her story became one of the best-selling sagas ever, proving that true game-changers are forged in the fires of adversity. Her quiet, persistent comeback is a reminder that while the spotlight may initially favor the superstars, the real impact comes from those who keep moving forward, no matter the odds.

In his unforgettable 2005 Stanford commencement speech[23] Steve Jobs revealed a profound truth: you cannot connect the dots looking forward. You can only connect them in hindsight. He recounted how dropping out of college wasn't a failure but a bold move to free himself from the rigid curriculum, allowing him to "drop in" on classes that truly inspired him. One such class was calligraphy, a subject he fell in love with despite having no practical plans at the time. Little did he know that this course would lay the foundation for the beautiful typography that would later transform how we experience computers, turning letters and words into art forms.

Jobs's story reminds us of every twist and turn in our lives. Every challenge, setback, and unexpected detour plays a crucial role in shaping our future success. For leaders, this philosophy is a powerful lesson: True innovation and lasting achievement are not born from a straight path but from embracing every experience, however random or

---

23 https://www.youtube.com/watch?v=Hd_ptbiPoXM&ab_channel=Stanford

difficult it may seem at the moment. As managers, we can instill this resilient mindset in 90% of our team daily. By encouraging them to see setbacks as vital pieces of a larger puzzle, we empower them to become true game changers, capable of transforming every challenge into a stepping stone toward success.

For every game changer who reshapes their world, hundreds, maybe thousands don't. The reasons for this vary: lack of opportunity, fear of failure, external circumstances, or simply giving up when the path becomes too difficult. But what separates those who break through from those who fade into obscurity? Why do some Hollywood actors become household names while others disappear after a handful of roles? Why do only a select few musicians earn a coveted spot in the Boston Symphony Orchestra while countless talented performers never get their shot? How does a platform like TikTok revolutionize social media while Vine, its predecessor, fades into irrelevance?

Perhaps the most telling example of this dynamic is Skype. For years, it was the dominant player in virtual communication. Yet, during the most significant moment in history for online meetings—the pandemic—it lost its crown to a little-known competitor: Zoom. How did the most established brand in video conferencing lose ground when demand had never been higher? The answer lies in one critical factor: adaptability. Zoom focused on seamless usability, faster connections, and fewer complications at a time when the world needed those things most. Meanwhile, Skype, weighed down by bureaucracy and stagnation, missed the moment—and in May 2025, Microsoft, the owner of Skype, closed down the platform.

Success and achievement are built through relentless effort, adaptability, and a willingness to push forward despite failures. The individuals and companies that succeeded were once part of the 90%: ordinary people, grinding away, facing setbacks, and questioning if they would ever break through. However, their persistence, resilience, and ability to evolve are what ultimately elevated them into the elite 10%. Those who succeed don't just dream, they take action, adapt, and persist when others would give up. They embrace challenges as opportunities, stay resilient through setbacks, and embody the mindset of a true game changer.

A Playbook for Leaders: Coaching Resilience and Building Game Changers

As we've established, while the spotlight often shines on top performers, the steady, dedicated efforts of the 90% keep the team moving forward and ensure lasting success. Confidence, a key driver of performance, doesn't come from natural talent alone. It is built through experience, consistency, and the ability to navigate challenges. As a leader, your role is to create an environment where both everyday contributors and high potentials can thrive by fostering opportunities for growth, reinforcing their value, and helping them develop the confidence needed to take ownership of their success.

One of my favorite keynotes to deliver is speaking with parents. An audience that, despite lacking a user manual for parenting, is always eager to learn how to do it better. These parents of competitive sports athletes often come in with grand visions of their child earning a D1 scholarship. (Newsflash: That rarely happens.) Recently, I addressed a room full of softball and baseball parents, all required to attend if they wanted their athlete in a specific club program.

At the start of the session, I ask about their goals for their child in baseball and softball. While scholarship dreams often surface, the more common aspirations are for their kids to have fun, learn the sport, and perhaps most surprisingly, build confidence. And then I ask: How exactly do you think playing baseball or softball builds confidence? With 20 years of coaching baseball and 15 in softball under my belt, I can tell you these sports are among the worst for boosting a player's self-esteem. Consider this: Even professional players, who earn millions, fail more than 75% of the time. A batting average of .300, meaning you fail 7 out of 10 times, is considered excellent. There is no other industry where you can succeed just 30% of the time and not only keep your job but be celebrated for it. Imagine a surgeon or airline pilot with those stats. So, if confidence is the goal, how will you prepare your child for life's challenges if you expect them to thrive on constant failure? If you're looking for guaranteed success, have them swim. At least when they dive off the board, they're guaranteed to hit the water.

That's when I pause momentarily and get serious, asking: Where does confidence come from? You cannot pick it up at a local store or acquire it by donning a particular outfit. True confidence is forged through persistent effort—by relentlessly striving to learn, grow, and improve. It comes when hard work pays off: When the goal is achieved, when the ball is hit. That tangible success, born out of continuous effort, is the real foundation of confidence.

Building genuine confidence isn't about shortcuts or quick fixes. It's the product of consistent effort, perseverance, and a commitment to growth. When leaders understand that true confidence is developed over time through overcoming challenges and celebrating small wins, they can cultivate a resilient, motivated team. With that understanding in mind, here are some ideas that can become your playbook for fostering resilience, motivation, and engagement across all team levels.

Recognize and Reinforce the 90%

Too often, the unsung heroes of an organization are only noticed when something goes wrong. Yet, they are the backbone of long-term success. As a leader, it's crucial to make a habit of acknowledging and highlighting their consistent contributions. Whether it's through direct recognition, public appreciation, or tying their efforts to larger organizational goals, showing them that their work matters keeps them engaged and motivated. When employees see the impact of their efforts, they become more invested in the team's success, strengthening the foundation of the organization.

> *"Building genuine confidence isn't about shortcuts or quick fixes. It's the product of consistent effort, perseverance, and a commitment to growth."*

Build Resilience Through Support, Not Just Pressure

Resilience isn't built through relentless pressure—it's fostered through a culture that views mistakes as learning opportunities rather than career-ending failures. Encouraging adaptive thinking helps employees navigate setbacks confidently while creating an environment of psychological safety, ensuring they feel comfortable taking risks, sharing ideas, and growing from their experiences. A leader's job is to guide their team toward what they can control rather than focusing and dwelling on obstacles. Employees who feel supported rather than judged develop the confidence to overcome challenges and perform at their best.

Engage and Elevate the 10%

High performers thrive on challenges and opportunities to grow. Keeping them engaged means offering meaningful, stretch assignments that push them to develop new skills. However, it's not just about challenging them—it's about creating mentorship opportunities that allow them to share their knowledge while also learning from others. Pairing high performers with members of the 90% fosters collaboration, strengthens the team, and helps cultivate future leaders. At the same time, leaders must be mindful of sustainability; even top talent needs balance to avoid burnout. Supporting their growth while ensuring a healthy workload allows them to sustain peak performance over the long term.

Coach Like a True Leader

The best leaders don't just manage—they coach. Being actively involved in your team's development means going beyond delegation and providing real guidance, feedback, and encouragement. Transparent communication fosters trust, clarifying expectations, challenges, and opportunities for employees. But above all, leaders must model resilience and adaptability in their own work. Employees take their cues from those at the top—if you demonstrate perseverance, optimism, and a solutions-oriented mindset, your team will follow suit. Leadership isn't about demanding excellence; it's about inspiring it.

Leadership Is a Long Game

The best leaders understand that their greatest impact isn't in managing the moment but in shaping their teams' long-term resilience and engagement. Success isn't just about developing the elite 10% or keeping the 90% motivated. It's about building a system where everyone, regardless of their role, is empowered to play their part, bounce back from setbacks, and contribute to lasting success.

Game changers aren't born. They are built. And great leaders are the ones who know how to develop them. Leaders create an environment where everyone can thrive by recognizing and reinforcing the contributions of the 90%, fostering resilience through support rather than pressure, and strategically engaging the high performers. Success isn't just about identifying talent; it's about cultivating it, providing the right challenges, and modeling the behaviors that drive growth. When leaders commit to this approach, they don't just build strong teams—they build a culture of resilience, adaptability, and continuous improvement. The true measure of leadership isn't in personal achievements but in the success of those you empower.

Laughter: The Secret Weapon of Resilience

If there's one thing I've learned from coaching, parenting, and watching my daughters play through pain—often while I downplayed their injuries with a clueless "Put some ice on it"—it's that resilience thrives where there's room for humor.

> *"Humor doesn't erase the hardship. It reframes it. It says this moment might be hard, but we're not going to let it beat us."*

Laughter isn't just a nice-to-have leadership trait. It is a game changer. When my daughter broke her finger and I kept insisting it was just a blood blister, we could have let it become a sore spot, literally and emotionally. But now, every time we see something go sideways, one of us will throw out "Yeah, but can you pitch?" and suddenly the tension breaks. Humor doesn't erase the hardship. It reframes it. It says this moment might be hard, but we're not going to let it beat us.

This is true on the field, at home, and especially at work.

When Saturday Night Live returned after 9/11, the country was desperate for healing. Lorne Michaels opened the show standing beside firefighters and first responders. With the nation still raw, he asked, "Is it okay to be funny?" The answer, dry and perfect: "Why start now?" That moment did not dismiss grief. It acknowledged it with humanity and gave us all permission to exhale.

The same principle applies in leadership. Humor diffuses pressure, builds connection, and sparks creative thinking. A well-timed joke during a tough meeting, a leader willing to laugh at their own misstep, or a team that can find joy even when the numbers are not hitting—that is not frivolous. That is the sign of a resilient culture.

Even comedy legends have something to teach us here. Robin Williams used improvisation and empathy to connect instantly with his audience, two qualities every great leader needs. George Carlin used wit to challenge assumptions. Steve Martin mixed intellect with absurdity to see problems differently. Eddie Murphy mastered the art of storytelling to turn everyday struggle into shared laughter.

That is leadership.

If you want your team to bounce back faster, innovate better, and stick together longer, teach them to laugh together. Create space for levity. Be the first to admit your mistake and joke about it. You are not lowering the bar. You are raising the team's emotional agility.

Because sometimes, right after the worst pitch, the best line you can deliver is, "Okay, but can you pitch?"

That is the heart of the 90% advantage. It is not about perfection. It is about showing up, shaking it off, laughing when you can, and doing your best. The real advantage belongs to those who keep going, who turn mistakes into momentum and missteps into moments of connection.

MILTON HERSHEY: SWEET RESILIENCE— A JOURNEY FROM SETBACKS TO TRIUMPH

Milton Hershey's passion for candy began early in life when he apprenticed with a local confectioner, immersing himself in the art of making sweets. This early exposure ignited a fascination with chocolate that would drive him to pursue greatness. Determined to break into the booming confectionery market, Hershey ventured to New York City, where he sought to capitalize on his passion for chocolate. However, the competitive and fast-paced environment of New York proved unforgiving.

In New York, Hershey faced a series of daunting challenges. Technical mishaps, production inefficiencies, and stiff competition plagued his early chocolate ventures. To fund his ambitious projects, he invested nearly all of his personal savings and took on loans, but the returns never materialized as expected. Mounting financial losses, reportedly amounting to a substantial sum, left him teetering on the brink of ruin. The pressure was immense—he feared that if his failures became public, not only would his career be over, but his mentors and backers might also suffer the consequences.

Eventually, forced to confront these harsh realities, Hershey made the difficult decision to abandon his New York dream and return to Pennsylvania—a place with familiar roots and a more supportive environment for his creative pursuits. In Pennsylvania, he took a radically different approach. Slowing down to meticulously refine his candy recipes, he invested in modern production techniques that allowed him to maintain tight quality control. The calmer, nurturing atmosphere enabled him to experiment and perfect his chocolate formula without the frantic pressures of New York. It was here that, after countless trials, Hershey finally experienced his breakthrough—the moment he realized he had created a chocolate product with the potential to captivate the nation.

The events of World War II further bolstered the timing of his success. As the war raged on, the U.S. government included Hershey's chocolate in soldiers' rations, exposing millions to his finely crafted creation. Demand skyrocketed, and Hershey rapidly scaled up production. Although he faced challenges such as supply chain disruptions and quality control issues during this expansion, his unwavering commitment to innovation and excellence allowed him to overcome these hurdles and secure his place in the industry.

Beyond building a chocolate empire, Milton Hershey was driven by a deep sense of social responsibility. Though he never had children of his own, he dedicated a significant portion of his wealth to philanthropic efforts. Hershey established the Milton Hershey School—a home and educational institution for underprivileged children—which continues to support thousands of foster and low-income youth to this day. His legacy lives on through the Hershey Trust Company and the ongoing work of the school, ensuring that his commitment to nurturing young lives and providing opportunities for success endures.

Milton Hershey's journey is a powerful testament to the transformative power of resilience, innovation, and a commitment to giving back. Though devastating, his early setbacks in New York taught him invaluable lessons about precision and perseverance. By returning to Pennsylvania and focusing on quality and consistency, he turned near ruin into a nationwide phenomenon. Hershey's legacy—marked by both monumental failures and triumphant breakthroughs—serves as an enduring reminder that even the bitterest challenges can lead to the sweetest successes, both in business and in the lives of those we touch.

LEADER'S PLAYBOOK

TURNING SETBACKS INTO COMEBACKS

Here are five practical ways leaders can coach resilience and inspire comeback-ready teams:

1. *Model recovery, not perfection.* When things go wrong (and they will), let your team see how you respond. Leaders who acknowledge mistakes, show how they regroup, and move forward give others permission to do the same.

2. *Reframe failure as feedback.* Normalize learning out loud. Use questions like "What's the opportunity here?" instead of "Who dropped the ball?" Reflection beats retribution.

3. *Look for the blood blisters.* Not every issue needs a full-blown intervention, but every issue deserves awareness. Pay attention to the smaller pains your team is managing before they fracture into something bigger.

4. *Build emotional agility.* Encourage your team to name frustrations, share setbacks, and then shift the story. Humor helps. So does a mantra like "Can you pitch?" to prompt resilience with levity.

5. *Reward grit.* Celebrate the quiet wins—the tough conversations had, the risks taken, the recoveries made. These are the real metrics of a resilient culture.

Great teams don't avoid adversity—they're equipped to respond to it. And great leaders provide the mindset, the modeling, and the language to bounce back better.

Because at the end of the day, leadership isn't about always having the perfect pitch—it's about having the courage to throw it anyway.

"You miss 100% of the shots you don't take."

— Wayne Gretzky

9.

Small Wins, Big Gains

True success isn't about raw talent or natural ability. If it were, we'd all be sitting on the couch waiting for our hidden genius to reveal itself. Instead, success is about persistence, discipline, and overcoming obstacles. Some of the most inspiring figures in history weren't the most gifted in their field, but they refused to quit. Michael Jordan was cut from his high school basketball team before becoming one of the greatest athletes ever. Imagine being the coach who made that call. Howard Schultz grew up in public housing and was rejected by over 200 investors before transforming Starbucks into a global brand. Proving that sometimes, all you need is a good idea and an unhealthy obsession with coffee. Oprah Winfrey overcame poverty and rejection early in her career before becoming one of history's most influential media personalities. Admiral William H. McRaven, best known for leading the operation that took down Osama bin Laden, emphasizes how small, disciplined actions, like making your bed each morning, build the resilience needed for greater success. Who knew that tidying up could be a secret weapon for world domination? These underdogs prove that resilience is the ultimate equalizer.

The strongest leaders, the most successful teams, and the most resilient organizations aren't those who avoid setbacks but those who embrace them. Learning to build momentum through small, strategic wins. True leadership isn't about grand, defining moments; it's forged in the daily grind, in the decisions made when no one is watching, and in the ability to adapt when circumstances don't go as planned. Legendary UCLA coach John Wooden didn't build a championship dynasty by focusing on championships. He built it by drilling his players on the fundamentals, down to how they laced their shoes. That's right, a man with ten NCAA championships under his belt started with shoelaces. The makers of Formula 409 understood this, too. Most people assume the name is a random number or a secret chemical code. It's not. It's called Formula 409 because it was the 409th attempt to get the formula right. They failed 408 times before landing on the right combination. That name is not just a brand. It's a badge of persistence. Thomas Edison famously reframed thousands of failed experiments as steps toward innovation, proving that resilience isn't just about endurance. It's about finding the lesson in every setback. Small, intentional actions compound over time, shaping those who refuse to let adversity define them and proving that success isn't about avoiding challenges but learning how to leverage them.

> *"Small wins are the building blocks of big victories. They create momentum, build confidence, and establish a culture where progress is both measurable and sustainable."*

Small wins are the building blocks of big victories. They create momentum, build confidence, and establish a culture where progress is both measurable and sustainable. This is where the 90% advantage comes into play. It provides the game plan and blueprint for harnessing the power of incremental success. Just as a football game isn't won by a single touchdown but by a series of well-executed plays, leadership, business, and personal growth rely on stacking small, consistent achievements over time. When managers recognize and elevate the everyday contributions of their team, the 90% who often operate outside the spotlight unlock untapped potential, drive engagement, and cultivate a high-performing environment. The 90% advantage isn't just a philosophy. It's a strategic approach that ensures steady progress, builds resilience, and turns seemingly ordinary efforts into extraordinary results.

Moving forward isn't about crossing a finish line. It's about embracing the process of continuous growth. Leadership, resilience, and success aren't destinations; they are disciplines built through deliberate choices, consistent action, and the ability to learn from every challenge. Each small win lays another brick in the foundation of something greater, reinforcing the habits that create lasting impact. The 90% advantage is more than a concept. It's a mindset that ensures progress even when the finish line keeps moving. The effort you put in today isn't just about meeting short-term goals. It's about shaping the future, stacking victories, and positioning yourself and those around you for long-term success. Because, in the end, the biggest wins aren't about waiting for a game-changing moment. They are simply the result of never stopping the work.

The Myth of Overnight Success: Why Winning is a Slow Burn

The idea of "overnight success" is one of the most misleading and frustrating myths in business, leadership, and life. It's the story we tell ourselves when someone rises to the top seemingly out of nowhere. Whether it's a startup founder selling their company for millions, an athlete breaking records, or an influencer skyrocketing to fame because they made a viral video of their cat playing the piano, if you dig a little deeper, you'll find that almost every "instant success" was actually years, if not decades, in the making. What appears to be a breakthrough moment is just the public unveiling of years of unseen work, failures, and persistence.

This myth thrives because we live in a world that only showcases results, not the grind behind them. Social media and headlines love a dramatic narrative where a person wakes up one day, launches an idea, and watches it explode in popularity. We rarely hear about the late nights fueled by bad coffee, the financial struggles that made them question their life choices, the rejections that felt like gut punches, and the countless times they nearly threw their laptop out the window. The truth is that most successful individuals spend years perfecting their craft, making mistakes, and learning hard lessons before they ever see tangible results. Yet, because we only witness their success at its peak, it can feel like they had some secret formula that propelled them there overnight. But they didn't.

> *"True success isn't about hitting a home run on the first swing—it's about consistently showing up, learning from setbacks, and making daily improvements that compound over time."*

This perception fuels jealousy and self-doubt. It's easy to compare our behind-the-scenes struggles to someone else's highlight reel and feel like we're falling behind. We question our own progress, wondering why things aren't happening as fast for us. "Why haven't I built a million-dollar empire yet? I've been working hard for at least three whole weeks!" The only difference between those who "make it" and those who don't is the willingness to keep going when no one is watching. The real work happens in the 90% of time that goes unnoticed. The hours spent refining skills, adjusting strategies, and pushing through obstacles make us want to curl up in the fetal position.

To overcome this myth, individuals must shift from chasing rapid success to embracing steady, intentional progress. It takes discipline, patience, and the ability to focus on small, incremental wins rather than waiting for a single defining moment. True success isn't about hitting a home run on the first swing—it's about consistently showing up, learning from setbacks, and making daily improvements that compound over time. And let's be honest, if every success story happened overnight; we'd all be CEOs of something by now.

When leaders stop idolizing overnight success and start valuing steady improvement, they empower their teams to thrive. They set the tone that success isn't about a lucky break but about commitment, learning, and perseverance. In doing so, they build organizations that not just chase momentary victories but cultivate a culture of sustained excellence.

The Participation Trophy Experiment: How We Got Here

At some point in the late 20th century, a generation of well-meaning parents looked at their children and thought, Let's make sure they never feel the sting of losing! And thus, the great Participation Trophy Movement was born. These parents had grown up in a different era. One where only the winners got medals, coming in last meant being teased and bullied, and coaches yelled things like, "Walk it off!" when a kid twisted an ankle. Determined to raise a kinder, more emotionally supported generation, they swung the pendulum in the opposite direction. Instead of rewarding just the top performers, they handed out trophies and multiple-colored ribbons to every child who laced up their sneakers, showed up to a race, or managed to stay awake through a game of T-ball.

The idea wasn't entirely ridiculous at first. The parents of Millennials had grown up in a hyper-competitive, often cutthroat environment, and they saw firsthand how losing could crush self-esteem. So they thought, "What if we remove that part? What if everyone gets a little recognition so no one feels left out?" On paper, it sounded like a brilliant way to build confidence. It created a generation of kids who learned that effort alone was enough to be celebrated. Even if they never actually scored a goal.

Fast forward a couple of decades, and those same Millennials, once showered in gold-colored plastic trophies, entered the workforce and got hit with a cold, hard truth. Real life does not hand out participation awards. Employers don't give raises for just showing up. Promotions aren't doled out for enthusiasm. And no one ever got recognized on a company-wide email for "trying their best." Suddenly, the safety net that was supposed to boost confidence started to feel like a trap. Millennials weren't unmotivated. They just had to rewire their understanding of success.

Unlike previous generations who prioritized stability and loyalty to a single employer, Millennials entered the workforce believing they could and should chase their dreams. They were the first generation raised with the idea that work should be fulfilling, not just a paycheck. Before the 2008 Great Recession hit like a wrecking ball, many Millennials kept their résumés updated on Monster.com even after landing a new job, always looking for something better. They weren't necessarily eager to put in long hours; they just expected promotions, perks, and purpose to come naturally. After all, they had been told since childhood that they were special and could be anything they wanted to be.

Then, the economy tanked, layoffs skyrocketed, and unpaid internships became the new normal. Reality hit hard, and Millennials had to adjust. Over time, they shifted from entitlement to resilience, redefining success on their own terms. While previous generations valued a steady paycheck and a corner office, Millennials wanted their work to mean something. They didn't just want to have a job. They wanted to believe in their job.

As Millennials settle into leadership roles, Generation Z is stepping into the workforce with an entirely new set of expectations. Born between the late 1990s and early 2010s, Gen Z is the first generation to have grown up entirely in the digital age. They never had to dial up to get online, they've been fluent in social media since middle school, and they have little patience for inefficiency in the workplace. They expect speed, transparency, and meaningful work. And, if they don't get it, they won't hesitate to update their LinkedIn and start job hunting.

Unlike Generation X, who spent years proving themselves through long hours and hustle, and Millennials, who entered the workforce with optimism and believe that work should be meaningful, Gen Z has taken a more pragmatic approach. Growing up watching Millennials struggle with student debt, economic downturns, and the false promise of "do what you love and the money will follow," Gen Z isn't easily convinced that passion alone pays the bills. They've witnessed instability firsthand and tend to be more financially cautious, prioritizing job security and flexibility. They also expect work-life balance, mental health support, and clear paths for advancement without believing that they must "pay their dues" for years before earning it. If those needs aren't met, they won't hesitate to find an employer who gets it.

And just when leaders think they've finally figured out how to engage the modern workforce, Gen Alpha is right behind them, bringing an entirely new set of workplace expectations. Born after 2010, these future employees have grown up in a world of AI assistants, personalized learning apps, and digital-first experiences. Unlike previous generations who had to adapt to new technology in the workplace, Gen Alpha will expect businesses to be built around them. Hyper-efficient, seamlessly integrated with technology and designed for instant feedback.

If Millennials wanted purpose and Gen Z wanted work-life balance, Gen Alpha will likely expect their careers to function like their favorite apps: intuitive, interactive, and optimized for their strengths. They won't just want feedback. They'll want real-time analytics on their performance, preferably with an interactive dashboard tracking their success. They'll expect learning opportunities to be on demand, career paths to be customizable, and workplaces to be designed around personal development.

So, what does this mean for managers? Leadership will need to be more adaptive than ever. Gen Z expects leaders to listen, collaborate, and provide real opportunities for growth. Gen Alpha will take that even further, expecting customization, gamification, and a workplace experience that feels as seamless as their social media feeds. The 90% advantage remains the best strategy for leaders navigating this evolving workforce. Whether an employee is a Millennial looking for purpose, a Gen Zer seeking balance, or a future Gen Alpha worker expecting their career to feel like a perfectly optimized mobile app, the key remains the same. Leaders who invest in their people, acknowledge small wins, and create an environment of continuous growth will always have the strongest teams.

For managers, this means shifting the focus from outdated ideas of success to a more practical, motivating approach. One that recognizes small wins emphasizes growth and provides real opportunities for development. The 90%

advantage is tailor-made for this kind of leadership. Instead of obsessing over the handful of top performers, great leaders invest in the majority. The ones who show up, do the work and want to improve. The lesson from the participation trophy era isn't that Millennials are entitled. It's that they respond best to a system where effort is acknowledged, improvement is encouraged, and success is earned.

And if they still want a trophy at the end of the day? Fine. But let's make sure it actually means something this time.

Small Wins, Big Impact: How the Little Things Add Up

Despite what highlight reels and social media feeds might have us believe, success is not built on sweeping, dramatic moments. It's rarely about a single game-winning shot, a billion-dollar idea scribbled on a napkin, or a viral breakthrough that changes everything overnight. Instead, real, sustainable success results from small, strategic victories that stack up over time—each one a stepping stone toward something greater.

A single push-up won't make you fit (unfortunately), reading one book won't make you a genius, and sending one email won't land you a promotion (though adding "Per my last email" might get you noticed). But do any of those things consistently; over time, they compound into measurable results. That's the power of small wins. Even the tiniest achievement creates momentum, fuels confidence, and makes the next step easier. The best part? Small wins are accessible to everyone every day.

Psychologists have studied this extensively. Research shows that our brains are wired to crave progress, no matter how minor (Atlassian, 2021)[24]. Completing a task, whether clearing out your email inbox or simply checking something off your to-do list, triggers the release of dopamine, the brain's feel-good chemical associated with motivation and reward. This is why video games are so addictive; they constantly give players small, achievable goals to keep them engaged. Imagine applying that same principle to leadership, business, or personal development. Leaders who understand the power of small wins don't just sit around waiting for a big breakthrough before celebrating—they recognize and leverage incremental progress to build momentum, boost morale, and inspire continued effort.

Great managers take this approach to energize their teams. Instead of setting massive, long-term goals that feel overwhelming, they break objectives into smaller, attainable milestones. They don't just say, "Let's increase sales by 50% this year." They say, "Let's make five extra calls today." They don't expect employees to master an entirely new skill overnight but encourage them to improve just one percent at a time. These small efforts lead to major transformations. Kind of like how that one plant in the office somehow grows even though no one ever waters it.

The 90% advantage thrives on this principle. Most employees may never have a high-profile moment or make an earth-shattering impact, but that doesn't mean their contributions don't matter. In fact, they are the backbone of any successful organization. When leaders recognize and

---

24   https://www.atlassian.com/blog/productivity/the-psychology-of-check-lists-why-setting-small-goals-motivates-us-to-accomplish-bigger-things

reward small victories, whether it's an employee who improved their efficiency, handled a tough client well, or contributed a fresh idea in a meeting. They create a culture where progress is continuous, motivation stays high, and individuals feel valued.

Managers who embrace this mindset create a workplace where recognition isn't just reserved for record-breaking moments. It's woven into the daily culture. One effective approach is personalized recognition, where leaders acknowledge individual contributions through handwritten notes, public commendations, or shout-outs during team meetings. Acknowledging an employee's creative solution or extra effort can go a long way in fostering motivation.

Team celebrations also play a crucial role. Whether it's a casual team lunch, a virtual coffee break, or a small office gathering, appreciating collective achievements fosters camaraderie and engagement. Plus, who doesn't appreciate an excuse for free food?

For a more structured approach, gamified rewards can make recognition even more engaging. Implementing a points-based system that rewards employees for consistent effort and milestone achievements can reinforce positive behaviors. These points can be redeemed for perks like gift cards, extra time off, or company swag, making everyday contributions feel valued. Visual showcases, such as a "Wall of Fame" in the office or a digital recognition board, highlight employee accomplishments and keep motivation high.

Importantly, recognition should go beyond just the top 10%. While high performers deserve celebration, lasting engagement comes from finding meaningful ways to acknowledge the consistent effort, growth, and grit shown by the 90%. Rewarding small wins, improvement, teamwork, and persistence ensures that everyone sees a path to being valued—not just the stars. After all, a team isn't carried by a few standouts alone. It thrives when everyone feels seen.

Finally, routine acknowledgment must be part of everyday operations. Simple check-ins during meetings, where employees share recent wins, no matter how small, help ensure that continuous progress is noticed and appreciated. The key is consistency. When managers make it a habit to celebrate small wins, they create an environment where employees feel valued, engaged, and motivated to strive for success.

The lesson is simple: the little things add up. The small efforts, the everyday choices, and the incremental improvements are what shape long-term success. Whether in leadership, business, or personal growth, mastering the art of small wins is the key to achieving something far greater than any single defining moment ever could. And if all else fails, at least you'll have a to-do list with a lot of satisfying checkmarks.

The 90% Advantage in Action: Turning Everyday Effort into Extraordinary Results

Great leaders don't spend their time waiting for a big, game-changing moment to happen. If they did, they'd sit around like a group of kids waiting for lightning to strike their lemonade stand. The real magic in leadership isn't in chasing the occasional grand slam. It's in recognizing the everyday efforts that keep the game going in the first place. That's the heart of The 90% advantage. It's about shifting focus from the flashy wins to the steady, consistent contributions that make success possible.

> *"The real magic in leadership isn't in chasing the occasional grand slam. It's in recognizing the everyday efforts that keep the game going in the first place."*

Leadership, like pitching, is about showing up pitch by pitch. You don't win games with one perfect throw—you do it by staying focused on the next one. The most important pitch isn't the one you just threw or even the one that got crushed over the fence. It's the next pitch. The one you're about to throw. That's where momentum lives. That's where growth happens. When leaders embrace that mindset and reward consistent effort, they unlock extraordinary results from the most overlooked players on the field.

Organizations aren't generally built by a handful of superstars—unless, of course, you are the New York Yankees. They are built by the people who show up, put in the work, and keep things moving forward, even when no one's cheering for them. It's the customer service rep who de-escalates a furious caller, the office manager who somehow keeps the supply closet stocked with exactly the right kind of pens, and the project lead who translates vague executive ideas into something the team can actually execute. These people aren't making headlines but making the company function.

To truly harness the 90% advantage, leaders must actively recognize and develop everyday contributions. And no, this doesn't mean handing out participation trophies or muttering a half-hearted "Nice job." It means being intentional. A quick shout-out in a meeting, a thoughtful thank-you note, or a meaningful investment in someone's development. These small actions show people that their effort matters. Recognition shouldn't be reserved for record-breaking wins. It should be woven into the fabric of the culture. When people feel seen, they don't just show up—they lean in, take ownership, and give their best.

A workplace that embraces the 90% advantage also creates resilience. Because not every employee will be the next CEO, and that's fine. Not every player on a team is the star player, but that doesn't mean the offensive line isn't crucial. When leaders stop focusing only on the occasional MVP and start developing the whole team, they unlock a deeper level of engagement, innovation, and productivity. Employees don't just work for a paycheck. They work for a place that makes them feel like they matter.

At the end of the day, the 90% advantage isn't just a management strategy. It's a shift in perspective. It's about understanding that success isn't about one big, defining moment but daily moments. It's about making sure that the people who keep the lights on, the wheels turning, and the coffee pot full know they're just as important as the ones landing the big deals.

Real success is not about waiting for some dramatic, once-in-a-lifetime breakthrough. It is about stacking the small wins, building on steady contributions, and recognizing that the key to extraordinary results isn't chasing the few at the top. It is in unlocking the potential of the many. And if that means handing out an occasional, well-earned trophy for "Most Reliable Printer Fixer," so be it.

A CASE STUDY

STARBUCKS THE "OVERNIGHT" SUCCESS TWO DECADES IN THE MAKING

Today, Starbucks is synonymous with coffee culture worldwide, boasting over 30,000 stores across the globe. However, its journey to becoming a household name was far from instantaneous. The company's path is a testament to perseverance, strategic evolution, and the power of small, consistent efforts leading to monumental success.

Founded in 1971 by Jerry Baldwin, Zev Siegl, and Gordon Bowker, the original Starbucks in Seattle's Pike Place Market didn't sell brewed coffee. Instead, it specialized in high-quality coffee beans and equipment. For over a decade, Starbucks remained a modest operation with a handful of stores, focusing on educating consumers about premium coffee. This slow and steady growth helped establish the company's reputation for quality, even though it remained relatively unknown outside Seattle.

In 1982, Howard Schultz joined Starbucks as Director of Retail Operations and Marketing. A pivotal trip to Italy inspired Schultz; he was captivated by the espresso bars' ambiance and the sense of community they fostered. He envisioned bringing a similar experience to the U.S., transforming Starbucks from a retailer of coffee beans to a café culture hub. However, the original owners were hesitant, fearing the loss of their core identity. Undeterred, Schultz left Starbucks in 1985 to start his own coffee chain, Il Giornale, which quickly gained popularity. This early success was a small but significant win, proving that Americans were ready for a different kind of coffee experience. Recognizing the potential, the original founders sold Starbucks to Schultz in 1987. This acquisition marked the beginning of Starbucks' transformation into the coffeehouse model we know today.

Throughout the late 1980s and early 1990s, Starbucks expanded steadily, opening new stores across the U.S. and refining its customer experience. Instead of focusing solely on rapid growth, Schultz and his team paid close attention to small but impactful details. Perfecting the brewing process, training baristas to create a welcoming environment, and carefully selecting store locations to maximize foot traffic. These seemingly minor wins, like ensuring consistent espresso quality and making every store feel like a "third place" between home and work, created a strong foundation for long-term success.

It wasn't until the mid-1990s that Starbucks experienced what many perceived as "overnight" success. The company's IPO in 1992 provided capital for expansion, and its aggressive yet strategic store openings helped Starbucks become a recognizable brand. But behind the rapid growth were decades of small, intentional decisions, fostering customer loyalty through free samples, experimenting with store layouts, and even introducing the now-iconic Starbucks cup sleeve to improve customer experience. Every small innovation and operational refinement contributed to Starbucks' ability to scale successfully without losing its core values.

Starbucks' story exemplifies how sustained effort, adaptability, and a willingness to evolve can culminate in extraordinary success. What appears as an "overnight" triumph is often the result of years of dedication, learning, and incremental progress. For leaders and entrepreneurs, Starbucks serves as a reminder that embracing the journey, with its challenges and gradual milestones, is essential to achieving lasting success. Sometimes, the biggest wins are simply the result of stacking up thousands of small victories over time.

STACK SMALL WINS FOR BIG IMPACT

Here are five ways leaders can use small wins to unlock big gains and ignite the 90% advantage in their teams:

1. ***Break Down the Big Stuff.*** Stop trying to motivate your team with Everest-sized goals. Instead of "Let's grow 50% by Q4," try "Let's win this week." Break large objectives into bite-sized milestones. Daily or weekly targets give your team something they can grab onto—without needing climbing gear or oxygen tanks.

2. ***Celebrate Progress Loudly and Often.*** Don't save your enthusiasm for the big finish. Cheer for the first draft, the first sale, the first client callback. Recognition doesn't lose its power when it's frequent— it gains it. A well-timed "Nice work!" can create more momentum than a year-end trophy collecting dust.

3. ***Make Recognition Personal, Not Performative.*** Forget the generic "Employee of the Month" template. Tailor your praise. Know what each person values—some want a public shout-out, others prefer a private thank-you or the sacred gift of early dismissal on a Friday. Recognition only works if it feels real.

4. ***Gamify the Grind.*** Want to turn repetition into motivation? Introduce micro-rewards and friendly

competition. Points, badges, team scoreboards—
even a "Random Acts of Awesome" Slack channel. When people can see their progress, they stay
engaged. Plus, who doesn't want to win a coffee gift
card for crushing a Tuesday?

5. ***Be the Leader Who Spots the Quiet Wins.*** It's easy
to notice the big closers or the breakout stars. But
the 90%? They're the ones solving problems before
they reach your desk, catching errors before they
cost you, and fixing the printer for the fifth time
this month. Notice them. Thank them. Make it
clear that steady wins still count.

Small wins aren't small, they're stackable. They create culture, sustain performance, and show your team that every
effort counts. Build a workplace where momentum is celebrated, not just milestones. Because when you make a
habit of winning the day, the year takes care of itself.

*"Nobody who ever gave his
best regretted it."*

— George Halas

Conclusion

The Power of Everyday Effort

Success is not about a highlight reel. It's not about the flashy moments, the standing ovations, or the one-time heroic efforts that get immortalized in motivational posters. The reality is that greatness—true, lasting success—is built in the moments that don't make headlines. It's built in the early mornings, the late nights, and the times when the only audience is a blinking cursor on a spreadsheet or an empty coffee cup staring back in silent judgment. As legendary football coach Vince Lombardi once said, "The man on top of the mountain didn't fall there." Success isn't luck or a single breakthrough moment. It results from showing up, putting in the effort, and doing the work when no one is watching.

> *"Success isn't determined by a single defining moment but by the work done when no one is watching."*

The Three Core Principles that I discussed at the outset of this book are at the heart of high performance: Master the leadership mindset, build strategic relationships beyond the scoreboard, and strengthen resiliency through adversity. These aren't just buzzwords designed to look good in a PowerPoint presentation. They are the foundation that separates those who merely clock in from those who truly contribute—those who embrace the 90% advantage.

Over nine chapters, with fundamental conversations in each, these core principles have been dissected, applied, and tested, all revealing one undeniable truth: success isn't determined by a single defining moment but by the work done when no one is watching. It's the steady, everyday effort of the 90%. The people who don't need constant recognition to keep pushing forward, handle challenges without fanfare, and put in the effort to move teams, businesses, and families forward.

While the spotlight might shine on the rare, game-changing moments, the true advantage belongs to those who consistently execute the plays that don't make the front page. The unspectacular but essential decisions, the unseen problem-solving, and the resilience to keep going even when progress feels invisible. That's what creates a lasting impact. The 90% don't wait for the perfect opportunity or the grand stage. They show up daily, understanding that real success is built in the moments between the big wins.

Office meetings would have been outlawed years ago if success were only about big, dramatic moments. The real work isn't in the grand gestures. The follow-ups, the quiet problem-solving, and the small but essential efforts prevent everything from going off the rails when chaos strikes. It's the people who step up without waiting for a round of applause, who understand that progress isn't always accompanied by a trophy, and who recognize that steady, consistent effort is what drives real results. The scoreboard may show the final tally, but the outcome is determined long before then. Through the unnoticed blocks, the extra yards, and the relentless push that transforms good intentions into real performance.

Teams, businesses, and families don't thrive because of a few headline-worthy moments. They succeed because of the people who show up daily, ready to do the work, tackle the challenges, and keep things moving forward no matter what obstacles arise. The ones who ensure the wheels keep turning, even when it would be easier to let them stall. The ones who stay committed, even when no one is watching.

This kind of effort rarely gets the spotlight. No one hands out trophies for staying composed under pressure, navigating office politics, or keeping a team on track when motivation is running on fumes. There's no viral video celebrating the person who ensures a project actually gets done while everyone else is still tossing around ideas. Yet, these contributions hold everything together and drive real success.

> *"Success, growth, and impact aren't built on one defining moment. They're built on the thousands of choices made each day."*

Here's what truly matters: the game is won in the details. The big, flashy plays might grab the attention, but the steady, reliable field goals rack up points and ultimately decide the outcome.

The Small Plays That Define Success

Everyone loves a game-winning touchdown in the final seconds. It's the moment that gets replayed, analyzed, and immortalized in sports history. But often, the final score isn't determined by a single, breathtaking play. It's the accumulation of small moments: the well-executed block that prevents a sack, the third-down conversion that keeps a drive alive, and the routine field goal that quietly adds three points to the scoreboard. At the time, these moments don't seem like much. But in the end, they're the difference between winning and losing.

Life works the same way. Success, growth, and impact aren't built on one defining moment. They're built on the thousands of choices made each day—the moments when effort is required, even when there's no applause. The decision to double-check your work, have the difficult conversation, and push forward even when exhaustion whispers that quitting would be easier.

No one delivers this truth better than Al Pacino's character, Coach Tony D'Amato, in Any Given Sunday. In one of the most powerful locker room speeches in sports movie history, he looks his battered and beaten team in the eyes and tells them exactly what stands between them and victory: "Life…is a game of inches. The margin for error is so small—one half-step too late or too early, and you don't quite make it. One-half second too slow or too fast, and you don't quite catch it."

He's not talking about talent or luck. He's talking about the accumulation of effort. Every yard gained, every inch fought for—those are what determine the outcome. He reminds them that those inches aren't given in football, just like in life. They are earned—through grit, persistence, and a willingness to do the unglamorous work that rarely makes the highlight reel.

And those inches? They don't come from grand gestures. They come from showing up when quitting would be easier, from putting in the work when nobody is clapping, and choosing to push forward when discouragement creeps in. Because when the clock runs out, it's not the single spectacular moment that wins the game. It's every small, unseen effort that came before it.

Your Effort Is the Difference

If you ever doubt whether your effort matters, let's be clear: The work you do—especially the work that goes unnoticed—is what keeps everything running. Your support, whether to your team, family, or community, creates bigger ripples than you realize. The effort you put in today might not make the highlight reel, but it is the reason success happens at all.

You don't have to be the star player to win. You don't need a standing ovation to make an impact. The truth is, most victories are earned long before anyone is around to acknowledge them. It's not about the grand gestures, the big speeches, or the dramatic moments that define success. It's the small, consistent efforts that add up over time.

> *"The effort you put in today might not make the highlight reel, but it is the reason success happens at all."*

The Shawshank Redemption is one of the most re-played movies on cable television, a film that audiences return to repeatedly. What started as a modest box office performer in 1994 has since become one of the most beloved and critically acclaimed films ever. Nominated for seven Academy Awards, including Best Picture and Best Actor for Morgan Freeman, it has only gained more appreciation over the years, consistently ranking at the top of greatest movie lists. Its legacy continues to expand, proving that its themes of perseverance, resilience, and hope are as powerful today as they were decades ago.

What makes The Shawshank Redemption so compelling isn't an explosive action sequence or a dramatic twist, it's one man's slow, quiet persistence. Andy Dufresne didn't escape from Shawshank Prison in a moment of brilliance or luck. He spent 19 years digging, inch by inch, with nothing but a rock hammer and unwavering determination. There were no shortcuts or grand displays of defiance—just methodical, deliberate daily work. He chipped away at that wall, fully aware that progress was painfully slow, but he never stopped. And in the end, that relentless, unseen effort led to his freedom.

Andy's journey is the perfect example of the 90% advantage. He didn't rely on talent alone or wait for the perfect opportunity. Despite overwhelming odds, he cultivated the right mindset, embracing patience, focus, and long-term vision. He didn't go at it alone, either. He built relationships beyond the scoreboard, earning the trust and respect of his fellow inmates, particularly Red, who ultimately plays a key role in his future. Most importantly, he demonstrated resilience, refusing to let setbacks, isolation, or despair derail him.

His story is a testament to the idea that real success is rarely immediate. The most meaningful victories come not from dramatic breakthroughs but from the quiet, consistent work that happens when no one is watching. It's not about waiting for the big moment. It's about committing to the daily effort and trusting that small actions will add up over time. Andy Dufresne may not have been the strongest, the fastest, or the most powerful, but he embodied the essence of the 90%. The everyday effort that leads to extraordinary results.

That's what everyday effort looks like. No grand applause, no instant gratification—just steady, determined progress that no one notices until it changes everything.

The same principle applies in life. Promotions aren't handed out because of one big project but because of years of consistent effort. Trust in relationships isn't built overnight but through hundreds of small, meaningful actions. And personal growth isn't achieved through a single defining moment but through daily choices to keep going, keep learning, and keep pushing forward.

It's an everyday effort. And that is what gives you the advantage.